MAI
Round 2

MAI
Round 2

New Global and Internal Threats
to Canadian Sovereignty

Tony Clarke and Maude Barlow

Published in 1998 by Stoddart Publishing Co. Limited
34 Lesmill Road, Toronto, Canada M3B 2T6
180 Varick Street, 9th Floor, New York, New York 10014

Distributed in Canada by:
General Distribution Services Ltd.
325 Humber College Blvd., Toronto, Ontario M9W 7C3
Tel. (416) 213-1919   Fax (416) 213-1917
Email customer.service@ccmailgw.genpub.com

Distributed in the United States by:
General Distribution Services Inc.
85 River Rock Drive, Suite 202, Buffalo, New York 14207
Toll-free tel. 1-800-805-1083   Toll-free fax 1-800-481-6207
Email gdsinc@genpub.com

02 01 00 99 98 1 2 3 4 5

Canadian Cataloguing in Publication Data

Clarke, Tony
MAI round 2: new global and internal threats to Canadian sovereignty

ISBN 0-7737-6021-0

1. Investments, Foreign – Canada.
2. Corporations, Foreign – Canada.
3. Investments, Foreign – Social aspects – Canada.
4. International business enterprises.
5. Investments, Foreign (International law). I. Barlow, Maude. II. Title.

HG5152.C533 1998   332.67'3'0971   C98-932256-4

Cover design: Angel Guerra
Computer layout: Kinetics Design & Illustration
Text design: Tannice Goddard

For information on the MAI, visit www.canadians.org

Printed and bound in Canada

To our Canadian and
international activist colleagues
in the struggle against the MAI

CONTENTS

Acknowledgements

In writing this book, we are beholden to a whole community of researchers, writers, and activists too numerous to name here, although we have included many of their important works in our suggested reading list at the end of the book. We do wish to especially thank seven people for recent analysis that has been particularly helpful in formulating our arguments here: John Dillon of the Ecumenical Coalition on Economic Justice, on the global casino; Steven Shrybman of the West Coast Environmental Law Association, on the constitutional and legal ramifications of investor-state clauses; international trade lawyer Barry Appleton, on NAFTA and water; Ottawa researcher Barbara Robson, on the bilateral investment treaties; Gary Neil of ACTRA, on the WTO magazine ruling; Michelle Sforza of Public Citizen's Global Trade Watch in Washington, on the April 1998 MAI text; and Mark Vallianatos of Friends of the Earth, on the International Monetary Fund and alternative policy tools.

As always, the staff of the Council of Canadians has been terrific and we especially want to thank Anna Dashtgard and Patricia Armstrong for constant support and assistance. We are grateful to Jack Stoddart for caring so much about this issue, and to Don Bastian and Marnie Kramarich for guiding us through the writing process with humour and good judgement. Our families have been wonderful and we want to thank them for their constant support.

INTRODUCTION

On the eve of the millennium, a great global struggle is being waged. At stake are the democratic rights of people in Canada and around the world. And this bloodless battle, taking place in the boardrooms and backrooms of international agencies and corporations, is placing Canadian sovereignty in greater danger than ever before.

Also at stake is the whole notion of "the commons," the idea that through our public institutions we recognize a shared human and natural heritage to be preserved for future generations. Everything left in the public realm is under assault. Governments around the world are rashly selling public assets to the private sector, leaving no area untouched: transportation and telecommunications systems; public health, welfare, education, and pensions; forests, waterways, and energy; roads, prisons, and culture — nothing is sacred. The United Nations reports a 70 percent increase in global privatization in 1997 over the year before. The beneficiaries of this sell-off are the handful of transnational corporations that have become so powerful that they are displacing nation-states as the dominant economic, political, and cultural forces of our time.

For at least twenty years, these global corporations have sought to protect their interests by establishing binding rules through international agreements. Their "freedom to trade" with few regulatory restrictions has now been largely secured through the North American Free Trade Agreement (NAFTA) and the World Trade Organization (WTO). Of far more importance to transnational corporations, however, are rules to protect their global direct investment interests from government regulation, since foreign direct investment (FDI) has become *the* way for corporations to expand their international presence and clout. The only way to secure such investment protection is to be given constitutional equality to nation-states in international law, a status which transnational corporations have been seeking relentlessly and which they thought they had secured when in the mid-1990s the Paris-based Organisation for Economic Co-operation and Development (OECD) undertook to negotiate a Multilateral Agreement on Investment (MAI). As home to the twenty-nine most powerful nations on earth, the OECD seemed like the perfect forum for the deal.

Written by the International Chamber of Commerce, the MAI would give private corporations not only the legal status of nation-states in every signatory country, it would also give them — and them alone — such powerful tools to enforce their newly acquired rights that governments would be compelled by law to safeguard corporate interests over those of their own citizens. But the treaty-building process became complicated when citizens in the individual OECD member countries got wind of the proposed treaty and mounted an unprecedented campaign of global opposition, causing government delegations to get bogged down in what seemed to be irreconcilable differences.

Many Canadians breathed a deep sigh of relief in April 1998 when the OECD announced a six-month moratorium on its latest attempt to conclude negotiations on the MAI. This was the second time the deadline had been missed and the trade ministers of the member nations had been summoned to Paris to try to break the logjam. When they failed, they returned home to ponder what had gone wrong and how to get the process back on track.

The Canadian media had two reactions. Some hailed it as a victory for grassroots activism and declared that the exclusive nature of global politics would never be the same again. Others condemned the opposition as a small band of radical Luddites who had frightened the Chrétien government into submission. All, however, have declared the MAI dead in spite of the fact that OECD secretary-general Donald Johnston (a Canadian) has promised to revive and ratify the deal in 1999. That the MAI is history has become the accepted wisdom in Canada — and it is wrong.

It is wrong for several reasons. The Canadian government insists that it is continuing to seek an MAI at the OECD; indeed, the proposed treaty's latest draft, which we examine in this book, is even worse than the earlier drafts and does not leave any room for the Canadian government to fulfil its promise that it can protect vital areas of Canadian sovereignty and still sign the deal.* As well, the quest for MAI-like powers for private global capital is not just situated at the OECD. We outline here the other global venues — which include the WTO, the International Monetary

---

* Readers wishing to examine the latest draft of the MAI may find it at the following web address: http://www.tradewatch.org. For information on the MAI from the perspective of Canadian activists, consult the web site of the Council of Canadians, www.canadians.org.

Fund, and the Free Trade Area of the Americas — currently seeking to expand their mandates in order to include similar investment protections for transnational corporations.

Further, MAI clauses are already in place in a number of existing trade agreements; as a result, Canadian sovereignty has been deeply compromised in several key areas. We expose in this book three recent very serious examples: looming water exports, the government's reversal on its ban on the gasoline additive MMT, and the threat to Canadian magazines. In each case we show that Ottawa is doing little or nothing to defend Canadian interests because it has surrendered much of its power under the international trade agreements it has already signed.

Most important to note, however, is that the MAI is not a stand-alone deal but a vital component of a long-term search by transnational corporations for international laws to protect their interests and supplant nation-state rule with what we call corporate rule. These powerful institutions are hardly going to pack up and back off at the first sign of opposition.

We have written this book because we believe that the global corporate power grab represents the most serious threat to democracy in the last fifty years, and we don't see any sign that our governments are able or willing to defend our interests against it. We also believe that citizens have a unique opportunity, having mounted one of the most effective global citizen campaigns in recent history, to take advantage of the MAI's temporary setback and put forward *our* alternatives to the MAI and economic globalization. We must demand that our governments bring the rule of law to global capital. Nothing less will do.

1

POWER GRAB

Every year, the world's corporate and political elite converge on a little Swiss village called Davos to congratulate one another on advancing economic globalization and to plan their next round of targets. Attending the World Economic Forum is the new global royalty — more than one thousand CEOs, the heads of state and senior government officials of over seventy countries, plus a smattering of selected media barons and academics. The main attraction of this event for politicians is the opportunity to persuade transnational corporations to invest in their countries. Corporate leaders get to rub shoulders with the highest decision-makers in the world and influence the economic and social policies of governments. William Thorsell, senior editor of *The Globe and Mail*, says that the future direction of the world is set every year in the private salons of Davos, largely out of sight of the world's public.

However, the February 1998 meeting was a little different.

Economic globalization was getting a bad rap. The financial crisis in Asia had just broken and globalization proponents were stunned. President Bill Clinton had recently been denied "fast-track" authority, which would have exempted his international trade deals from the clause-by-clause scrutiny of Congress; this denial was a huge political loss for him and the globalization agenda. And ordinary people around the world were reacting strongly to the dismantling of their environmental, labour, and social standards in the name of global competitiveness. The movers and shakers of the Forum decided they had a public relations problem on their hands and invited participants to address the negative "optics" of this backlash, lest they derail the globalization train.

Canada's trade minister, Sergio Marchi, was in the midst of a bruising scrap with Canadian workers, environmentalists, and cultural nationalists over the proposed Multilateral Agreement on Investment, and he admitted in a speech to the Forum that his government hadn't done a good job of selling the "benefits" of the proposed deal at home. Trying to explain the massive opposition to the MAI from all over Canada, he said that the issue had become a cross-country shopping cart into which Canadians were putting largely unfounded anxieties about the future.

Marchi was partly right. The MAI had come, in fact, to represent something larger than itself, a tangible focus for anger over the recent decades of cuts, downsizing, lost jobs, lower living conditions, and assaults on the environment. It fast became a metaphor for the whole anti-human value system behind economic globalization and provided an opportunity for citizens in Canada and around the world to start to take back democratic control of their lives. But Marchi was also wrong. The anxiety

so many Canadians were experiencing was not unfounded para-
noia to be mollified with a little well-placed PR. Rather, citizens
had correctly concluded that in economic globalization, they had
been sold an ideological bill of goods of which the MAI repre-
sented the last outrageous straw.

Laying the Foundation

In the last twenty years, the growth of transnational corporations
that operate outside of any national or international law has
restructured the entire power order of the world. The top two
hundred corporations are now so big that their combined sales
surpass the combined economies of 182 countries and they have
almost twice the economic clout of the poorest four-fifths of
humanity. Their profits are escaping nation-state law and citizens
are being left to shoulder the burden as stateless traders abandon
their countries of origin. An estimated $2 trillion in financial
speculation moves around the globe every day in the global
trading markets, untouched and untouchable by governments.

An entrenched underclass is growing in every country of the
First World, as is an elite class in the Third — creating a global
South and North no longer related only to geography. The
United Nations reports that the disparity in the level of income
between the top 20 percent and the bottom 20 percent of the
world's population is 150 to 1 — double the figure of thirty years
ago. As countries line up one after another to privatize their
social security in the name of global competitiveness, they are
disenfranchising their millions of citizens who are left with no
social programs, health care, or access to education.

These corporations, however, are not just economic entities.
They are increasingly politically organized within and across

nation-states. Their interests have become national priorities for governments, which are rewriting social, economic, and environmental policy to ensure the health and growth of these corporations — and relinquishing national sovereignty in the bargain. However, corporate leaders know that there is a growing citizen backlash against them and that it is possible governments with different allegiances could be elected in the future. Their most urgent priority is, therefore, the development of a system whereby international trade and investment treaties secure their global status permanently and in law.

On the trade side, the creation of the most powerful international body on the planet, the World Trade Organization, was a significant milestone. Spawned at the conclusion of the Uruguay Round of the General Agreement on Tariffs and Trade (GATT) in 1995, the WTO was mandated by its 132 member countries to work toward the elimination of all remaining tariff and non-tariff barriers to the movement of capital and goods across nation-state borders. Its central mandate is to promote global free trade, period. It contains no minimum standards to protect the environment, labour rights, social programs, or cultural diversity.

What makes the WTO so powerful is that, unlike any other global institution, it has both the legislative and judicial authority to challenge laws, policies, and programs of countries that do not conform to WTO rules and strike them down if they can be shown to be "trade restrictive." Recently, American laws to protect Asian sea turtles from shrimp nets and dolphins from drift nets used to catch tuna off the coast of Mexico have been successfully challenged at the WTO. Once a WTO ruling is made, worldwide conformity is required. A country is obligated to harmonize its laws or face the prospect of perpetual trade sanctions.

An international agency, the Codex Alimentarius, sets global food standards on allowable pesticide, additive, and contaminant levels, as well as the labelling of genetically altered foods. If any country establishes a higher standard for any food product than that set by the Codex, it can be challenged under the WTO for trade violations. Sitting on virtually every committee of the Codex are representatives of the largest food and chemical transnational corporations in the world. The WTO has also thrust agriculture suddenly and brutally into the international free trade arena; any marketing or regulatory system that affects international trade in any way can now be classed as a barrier to trade.

What transnational corporations do not yet have, however, and what they most desire, is a set of global rules to protect foreign direct investment (FDI) — investment that penetrates international boundaries and requires a physical presence in the host country. FDI has expanded exponentially in the last two decades, and is now growing twice as fast as the trade in goods and services. Its importance to the bottom line of global companies is paramount. Although the U.S. had been seeking rules to protect the overseas investments of its corporations since just after the Second World War and had been pushing hard for rules to be adopted during consecutive rounds of the GATT, it wasn't until Canada capitulated in the North American Free Trade Agreement that rules to protect the FDI interests of global capital were incorporated for the first time into an international treaty.

Under NAFTA, Canada agreed to abandon screening of new American investment and takeovers of Canadian companies involving less than $150 million. American corporations were given "national treatment" rights, whereby they must be treated no differently than domestic companies, and NAFTA required the Canadian government to stop setting many "performance requirements," such as requiring an American company to achieve a level of domestic content, to balance exports and imports, to transfer technology to Canada, or to keep any profits in Canada in exchange for locating here. In other words, NAFTA guaranteed U.S. corporations almost full access to the Canadian economy. As well, NAFTA established the long-sought-after principle of "most favoured nation" for American corporations, which gave them equal treatment and access to the Canadian market, regardless of their labour, environmental, or human rights records outside of Canada.

NAFTA's most important feature, and the cornerstone of the future MAI, was the establishment of stringent compensation standards in the event of expropriation or nationalization, enforceable before an international trade tribunal. This meant that if the Canadian government wanted to protect old-growth forests already earmarked for clearcutting by an American transnational, or set up a national, public child-care program, it might have to pay compensation to foreign investors against lost future profits.

Going for the Gold

With the newly minted NAFTA as the prized prototype, the U.S., Europe, and Canada (a recent and fervent convert to economic globalization) decided that such investment rules would be good for the world — next stop, the WTO and the OECD. At the very first ministerial meeting of the WTO in Singapore, in December 1996, the contentious issue of a full Multilateral Agreement on Investment was forcefully advanced by First World countries and almost as forcefully rejected by Third World countries who saw the treaty as a new and potentially virulent strand of colonialism.

As a compromise, a working group was set up to study the issue further.

The MAI proposal was faring much better at the OECD, however; after all, its member countries house 477 of the Global Fortune 500 corporations. It is in the OECD's perceived self-interest to set aggressive rules to protect the investment interests of its home-based companies, especially in the developing world, where labour and environmental standards are low and where they might have the greatest problems with reformist governments in the future. The plan was to secure a "high-standard" agreement at the OECD to take back as a *fait accompli* to the WTO, where it would be very difficult for developing countries to resist.

The high-standard agreement being discussed at the OECD had been drafted by the International Chamber of Commerce and was a transnational corporation's dream. For the first time in history, a treaty would confer nation-state status on all corporations (called private investors); their global constitutional rights would now be fully enshrined in law. The agreement would include "national treatment" and "most favoured nation" clauses similar to those in NAFTA, but applied to a far greater number of countries and a far wider set of criteria. The definition of investment in the OECD MAI included contracts, intellectual property rights, patents, claims to money, real estate, government concessions and licences, government procurement, portfolio investment, currency trading, subsidies to health care, education, child and elder care, the arts and culture, and natural resources. By signing the MAI, nation-states would cede the right to regulate foreign corporations in all of these areas.

Further, the OECD MAI established clear rules by which governments would have to abide when dealing with all corporations, foreign and domestic. It would forbid governments to set performance standards such as affirmative action, community reinvestment, domestic content, local hiring, employment of nationals in senior positions, transferral of technology, or balancing of imports and exports; and the new rules would be retroactive, forcing governments to break previously signed contracts. In essence, governments would agree to give up forever the right to lever jobs and other benefits to the local community or the national economy from transnational corporations in exchange for access to publicly owned resources. Then these companies could repatriate 100 percent of the profits they made in one country back to their head office in another.

As well, the MAI set out clear rules for governments when they privatize a public asset, whether it be a natural resource, a prison, or a social program. Governments could no longer give preference to domestic buyers when selling a public asset but would have to open up every phase of the privatization process to transnational corporations. Wherever there was a mix of public and private funding for social, education, or health programs, the MAI would allow challenges by foreign investors, who could claim that public dollars skewed the "level playing field" promised them in the deal.

Most important, the OECD MAI would give transnational corporations power tools to enforce their newly established rights. They could sue governments directly for cash compensation in retaliation for introducing any new law, regulation, or practice, or even enforcing any existing law, regulation, or practice not evenly enforced in the past, that reduced the profits these corporations could reasonably have hoped to earn in their absence. The disputes would not have to be settled in the courts of the country being challenged; the corporations could choose an international arbitration panel operating under the auspices of such institutions as the International Chamber of Commerce. The proceedings would be held in secret; no environmental, labour, human rights, or other citizens' groups would have access to the process; and the decisions would be binding.

In creating this regime, the MAI would represent a truly radical departure from the norms of international law. It would provide corporations with the right to directly enforce an international treaty to which they are not parties and under which they have no obligations. It would be entirely one-sided; neither citizens nor governments could sue the corporations back. The MAI would provide foreign investors with new and substantive rights with which they could challenge government programs, policies, and laws all over the world.

Finally, the OECD MAI contained two clauses to limit the abilities of governments to exempt themselves from these onerous conditions. "Standstill" dictates that governments must refrain from passing any future law that violates MAI rules. Countries agree to list all their existing non-conforming laws and practices, to impose no new ones, and to make no amendments to existing ones. "Rollback" requires governments to eventually eliminate those laws and practices, including those they have listed as "country-specific reservations." In other words, with time, all government laws and practices are intended to be covered by the full terms of the MAI. And once a country signs on to the MAI, it is locked in for twenty years.

These were the essential elements of the global treaty the delegations of the OECD member countries were negotiating from early 1995. Almost no one — including politicians — outside of a few bureaucrats in the finance and trade departments of the various countries knew such talks were going on. By spring 1997, negotiators had agreement on 90 percent of the text and only missed concluding it that year because some minor areas still had to be worked out. They are probably sorry now. For the secrecy that surrounded these talks was about to be blown wide open and nothing about the MAI would be the same again.

A Date with Democracy

After being alerted to the MAI by the Third World Network (a coalition of hundreds of citizen advocacy groups in Southeast Asia), labour, environmental, and social activists in Europe, the U.S., and Canada started asking their governments about the nature of the mysterious global treaty. They could get no hard confirmation of the negotiations until Canadian activists came into possession of the actual text and circulated it to their counterparts around the world. Within months, citizens' groups in at least a dozen countries were launching public education campaigns against the MAI, and the cultural community and environmental organizations were spreading the word in their sectors and beginning to network with their cohorts in the other OECD countries.

Alarmed by the growing backlash, OECD officials invited a number of citizens' groups to meet with the MAI negotiating committee in October 1997. More than seventy major environmental, labour, and social groups converged on Paris and sent emissaries to the meeting at the stately mansion that houses the OECD. It became clear that there was no room for compromise on the part of the officials; they had their marching orders and only sought a "dialogue" with citizens' groups to try to head off the opposition that was building back in their home countries. After the OECD consultation, the groups came together and hammered out a strongly worded joint statement that would be endorsed by many hundreds of groups in sixty-eight countries around the world.

The statement slammed the process for its lack of consultation with civil society and said that the resulting text was completely unbalanced, elevating the rights of investors far above those of governments, local communities, citizens, workers, and the environment. It bemoaned the lack of enforceable obligations for corporate conduct and said the MAI would be in direct conflict with many existing and future laws and regulations that protect the environment, public health, culture, social welfare, and employment laws. "As the MAI stands, it does not deserve to gain democratic approval in any country. All the groups signing this statement will campaign against its adoption unless [major changes cited to the OECD negotiators the day before] are incorporated into the body of the MAI." The group then called a press conference, where it published this statement, announced the formation of a global campaign to stop the MAI, and then headed out to take the fight back home.

One of the first things the national campaigns did was get the information out to levels of government other than the national and to government ministries other than just finance and trade. Subnational governments became alarmed at the fact that they would be fully bound to the MAI but hadn't been consulted about it and officials in the departments of the environment, labour, health care, social services, education, and natural resources at all levels of government started demanding more information on the impact any such deal would have on their policies and programs.

To calm the public's fears about the MAI and its potential impacts, government delegations began to pile on reservations designed to provide temporary protection for certain laws, policies, and programs. During the six months prior to the new April 1998 deadline, the number of reservations filed by member countries more than doubled, from six hundred to over 1,300, creating a tight bottleneck in the negotiations. As well, countries that were really feeling the heat from their citizens, like Canada, France, and Australia, started asking to be exempted from core elements of the deal altogether, thus causing dissension inside the talks.

By January 1998, the demands for sector protection by individual countries were so strong that BIAC — the Business and Industry Advisory Committee to the OECD — blasted the negotiators; the committee implied, within the bounds of diplomatic language, that it might be better to have no deal at all for the time being than a deal that could be construed to offer protection to workers and the environment. It was also becoming apparent that the Clinton Administration was not confident that it could convince Congress to adopt this controversial treaty in 1998, after losing its bid for a renewal of fast-track authority in late 1997. The tension was not helped by the insistence of Canada and Europe that the U.S. repeal its trade sanctions legislation (such as the Helms-Burton Act against Cuba) and guarantee that it would not push for such provisions to be included in the final MAI.

A confidential report from a member of the Canadian delegation showed that by the OECD MAI negotiating meeting in February, the internal process was becoming acrimonious. Chairman Franz Engering was so upset he "relapsed into evangelism" to try to save the talks and the delegates found "ample blame to go around for this melancholy state of affairs." The chair and the secretariat of the OECD were castigated for "repeated fundamental errors in the management of the negotiation" as "any postponement of conclusion beyond April without 'some' agreement on key issues would result in a loss of momentum and in conceding victory to MAI opponents."

In March, the European Parliament passed a resolution (437 for, eight against), urging its members to reject the MAI in its present form. Rumours swirled around the March meetings that the MAI was dead, rumours that OECD deputy secretary-general Joanne Shelton (an American) hastened to deny. "Yes, there is a time problem," she said. "This is simply proving more complex than thought at the beginning. Every agreement is toughest at the end." No one could predict what would happen when the trade ministers of the OECD countries were summoned to Paris in April 1998 to try to break the impasse.

But one thing was certain. The secret nature of these talks was a thing of the past. Gone were the days when a handful of trade bureaucrats could meet in posh surroundings to create global agreements that would override democratic laws. The genesis of a powerful international citizens' movement was being formed and there would be no turning back now.

2

SHELL GAME

By the time the BMWs and Mercedes Benzes rolled through the gates of the old Rothchild palace in the 16th district of Paris early on the eve of April 27, 1998, to pick up the OECD delegates for their ministerial meeting, it had become clear that the MAI negotiations were stalled.

The meeting was turning out to be a public relations nightmare. This was the second time the OECD negotiators had failed to meet their own deadline for completing the MAI. Just moments before the ministers' limousines departed, former Liberal cabinet minister and now OECD chief Donald Johnston told the international press corps that much of the blame for the delay lay with the "misinformation campaign" being promoted by MAI opponents.

Shortly after Johnston's press conference, a battle began to brew among the chief negotiators who were meeting to hammer out a consensus on the final wording of the next day's ministerial communiqué on the MAI. The U.S. had proposed that formal negotiations resume in July 1998 without setting an official deadline for agreement. France countered with a demand that there be a six-month suspension of negotiations to allow governments to communicate and consult with their citizens.

The battle between the MAI negotiators reportedly lasted until 4:00 a.m. Normally, the powerful U.S. position would have won hands down. But France was more or less backed by other countries who were feeling heat over the MAI negotiations, including Austria, Belgium, New Zealand, and Canada. Although France won this round, the final wording of the communiqué gave the U.S. plenty of room to spin its own interpretation that a "pause" did not mean that negotiations would cease. As far as the U.S. was concerned, informal talks would continue.

After the ministerial meeting, when reporters asked Canada's trade minister Sergio Marchi what he thought about France's proposal for a "suspension" of the talks, he emphasized the need for "redemption" — not necessarily for the MAI itself, but more specifically for the poor way in which both his government and the OECD had handled it. Before leaving Ottawa for Paris, Marchi had been publicly critical of the way in which the OECD and its 1,500 staff members had handled both the negotiations and the task of communicating the MAI's purpose and contents to the public at large. Later that summer, his government would launch a consultative process with several sectors of Canadians, including environmental groups, labour unions, and municipalities.

To be sure, the MAI had been damaged by public opposition and further delays, but it was still very much alive. As Johnston declared a few days later: "It's not a question of 'if,' but 'when.'" Indeed, the main strategy of the proponents was to revive the

MAI. Just over two weeks later, for example, on May 16, the U.S. and the European Union announced that a compromise had been reached on the controversial Helms-Burton issue, which had been one of the major roadblocks in the MAI negotiations. While it later became evident that this particular conflict between the EU and the U.S. may not have been completely resolved (i.e., U.S. officials merely agreed to propose some minor amendments to the Helms-Burton law, changes which observers say have little or no chance of passing Congress), there was a great deal of public fanfare about the compromise, leaving the perception that the MAI negotiations were back on track.

Meanwhile, France insisted that the six-month pause be fully respected and that all negotiations on the MAI be suspended until October. To ensure this, French officials blocked the ratification of Germany's Lawrence Shomerus as the OECD's incoming chair of the MAI negotiations, thereby preventing any official action from being taken. But official suspension of formal negotiations did not necessarily eliminate the possibility of informal "underground negotiations," a favourite ploy of the U.S. For example, when formal talks at the WTO over the Financial Services Agreement were suspended after they ran into major obstacles in 1997, the U.S. negotiators went underground with a series of bilateral meetings, using whatever arm-twisting tactics were necessary in order to surface several months later with a "done deal."

Although it appears that U.S. officials have refrained from aggressively deploying this strategy again during the French-inspired MAI pause, there have been informal bilateral meetings set up to discuss and resolve some of the controversial issues. During the first full week of July 1998, for example, Joe Popovich, a high level official in the office of the U.S. Trade Representative in Washington, flew to Ottawa to meet on other issues, but used the occasion to meet informally with negotiators from the European Union and Canada on the MAI agenda. The meeting reportedly focused on two controversial issues: the EU's objections to the U.S. insistence that the MAI rules on government subsidies and procurement programs not apply to their federal and state practices; and the U.S. objections to the EU's insistence on a clause designed to protect the union's own provisions for economic and social integration among its member countries. While Popovich dismissed the purpose of the Ottawa meeting as simply "clearing cobwebs," the MAI talks were already being revived.

Indeed, despite France's objections, steps were being taken throughout the summer of 1998 to resume negotiations at the OECD. As part of a new offence, the OECD launched a publication entitled *Open Markets: The Benefits of Trade and Investment Liberalisation,* which reasserted the rationale behind the MAI. In the Netherlands OECD officials piloted so-called "dialogue sessions with civil society," and informal consultations were initiated with a number of international environmental organizations to entertain the idea of including new environmental language in the MAI. On June 26, the OECD began the formal revision of its voluntary Guidelines on Multinational Enterprises (which may be appended to the MAI) and on July 13, a formal meeting of OECD member countries was convened in London to discuss the proposed MAI accession clause, which would be used to get non–OECD member countries to sign on to the deal.

But the OECD is not the only place where the MAI is alive and kicking. During the spring of 1998, there were signs indicating that MAI-like provisions were popping up as major agenda items in other global organizations negotiating trade and finance issues. "The MAI has become a shell game," quipped Mike Dolan of Public Citizen's Global Trade Watch in the U.S. "Like the old game of trying to find the rotten pea under several walnut shells, the MAI keeps popping up — at the World Trade Organization, the International Monetary Fund, the Free Trade Area of the Americas . . . you name it!"

World Trade Organization

Initially, the European Union favoured the WTO over the OECD as the political venue for negotiating a global investment treaty. In fact, for the EU, a multilateral investment agreement was needed as the centrepiece of the newly formed WTO. "Investment," declared Leon Brittan as vice-president of the EU, "the most important theme of all for the future of the world economy . . . seems to me *the* top priority for the WTO in the years ahead . . . because it involves the development of an appropriate framework of binding rules." Although the developing countries were successful in putting the agenda on the back burner at the first ministerial meeting of the WTO in December 1996, the promoters of a global investment treaty had never given up on their plan to consolidate MAI-like powers in the WTO.

Just over a year later, when the MAI negotiations at the OECD ran into troubled waters, Canada's Sergio Marchi began to revive the idea that the WTO would be a more appropriate venue to complete the process. By the time the OECD ministerial meeting took place in April 1998, Canada and several European countries were openly promoting a transfer of the MAI to the WTO, claiming that it was a more inclusive body for negotiating a global investment treaty because its membership involved developing as well as developed countries. The official ministerial communiqué coming out of the April OECD meeting referred to work being done at the WTO on investment issues and also listed a number of developing countries that would be invited to be participants in the next round of negotiations in Paris.

But this did not mean that most developing countries in the South were in favour of shifting the MAI negotiations to the WTO. According to Martin Khor of the Third World Network, shifting the MAI negotiations to the WTO could have disastrous consequences for developing countries. Not only is the WTO designed to address trade rather than investment issues, but its power structure is heavily weighted against the interests of the developing countries. And when the United Nations Conference on Trade and Development (UNCTAD) brought together ambassadors from various Third World countries in June 1998 to talk about the MAI, including its possible transfer to the WTO, there was considerable resistance expressed based on negative experiences with foreign direct investment. What was needed, some argued, was another model whereby investment was made to serve the development priorities of countries and their peoples.

By July 1998, there were signs that even U.S. negotiators were moving away from their hardline position against negotiating the MAI at the WTO. Washington has consistently argued that a "high-standard" investment treaty could only be negotiated among like-minded industrialized countries at the OECD, and that negotiating at the WTO would result in a "watered-down" MAI. But when U.S. negotiators Joe Popovich and Alan Larson met with U.S. citizens' groups on July 15, they declared: "We'll do the investment deregulation elsewhere — we'll take it to the WTO, FTAA, etc." In effect, they said that if the MAI negotiations at the OECD are not completed during the next six to nine months, the U.S. would then support the move to the WTO.

Hemispheric Trade Regimes

The WTO is not the only shell harbouring the MAI pea. Throughout 1998, it has become more apparent that top priority is being given to incorporating MAI-like investment rules and disciplines in the major hemispheric free trade regimes that are currently taking shape around the world. They are, namely, the Asia Pacific Economic Cooperation (APEC), the new Free Trade Area of the Americas (FTAA), and the proposed Transatlantic Economic Partnership (TEP).

In April 1998, negotiations began on the establishment of the FTAA, a hemispheric free trade zone encompassing North and South America. The proposal for an FTAA was initially approved at the first Summit of the Americas in December 1994 when U.S. president Bill Clinton brought together the leaders of thirty-two countries (i.e., North, Central, and Latin America, plus the Caribbean), including Jean Chrétien. At the top of the FTAA agenda is the creation of a hemispheric Convention on Investment which is expected to cover a range of MAI-like rules and disciplines. To date, the draft proposals for the Convention include national treatment clauses, a ban on performance requirements, and expropriation protections. It is likely that government regulation of the inflows and outflows of capital will be eliminated in favour of what the documents call "full and free" repatriation of capital, profits, and dividends. While not all of the components have as yet been put on the table, negotiation sessions starting in September 1998 were designed to take the investor-state dispute settlement mechanism of NAFTA and expand it, for FTAA purposes, to include MAI disciplines. After all, the FTAA is essentially intended to be an extension of NAFTA, the place where the idea of an investor-state mechanism was originally conceived.

After the May 1998 G-8 Summit meeting in Birmingham,

British prime minister Tony Blair and Bill Clinton met to lay the groundwork for negotiations to establish a Transatlantic Economic Partnership between the European Union and the United States. Although the TEP is designed to create a free trade zone in goods and services between the U.S. and the EU, including liberalization of government procurement and intellectual property measures, the underlying priority will be to strengthen investment protection. In late March, however, the chief architect of the TEP proposals, Leon Brittan, was publicly challenged by French finance minister Dominique Strauss-Kahn for including MAI-like investment disciplines in the EU–U.S. negotiations. "What goes for the Multilateral Agreement on Investment goes for this treaty," he said, referring to France's strong objections to the MAI rules affecting culture. Earlier, French president Jacques Chirac had warned that Paris would not hesitate to block the proposed partnership. But by mid-May, France's protest had been tempered. On May 16, U.S. and EU negotiators hammered out their compromise agreement on how to handle the EU objections to the Helms-Burton law and how to work toward a settlement on culture. A key piece of the May 16 compromise was a joint EU–U.S. proposal calling for tougher measures in the MAI against the expropriation of private property.

Investment protection is also expected to be a major priority on the agenda of the APEC Summit scheduled for Malaysia in November 1998. However, APEC's approach to the liberalization of trade and investment differs from that of the other hemispheric regimes. Unlike the FTAA or the TEP, APEC does not employ a rules-based model for trade and investment. Instead, APEC was originally designed to be more of a consultative forum on what can be done to accelerate free trade and economic liberalization. But this does not mean that MAI-like investment protection measures are excluded from the APEC agenda. On the contrary, Canada and the other member countries (or "economies," as they are called in APEC) submit an Individual Action Plan which includes a progress report on what steps are being taken to strengthen protection for corporations and their investments. What these progress reports reveal is that many of the APEC member countries are beginning to introduce MAI-like rules and disciplines for protecting foreign investment along with target dates for their implementation.

International Monetary Fund

International trade organizations are not the only players in the MAI shell game. In March 1998 it became clear that global financial institutions like the International Monetary Fund (IMF) were also preparing to adopt part of the MAI agenda. In the heat of the Asian financial crisis, the IMF policy-making body (known as the Interim Committee) endorsed a proposal to broaden its mandate. Currently, the IMF has controls over a country's payments with regard to trade transactions in goods and services (known as current accounts). By amending its Articles of Agreement, the IMF would take control over investment funds flowing in or out of a country (known as capital accounts). In other words, the IMF would have the authority to permit investors to take any kind of capital in or out of a country, in any volume or at any time.

A main objective of the MAI is to establish the "right" of foreign investors to move capital in and out of countries without being subjected to government scrutiny or regulation. One of the ways in which governments can offset the destabilizing effects of short-term speculative investments is by regulating capital flows.

Chile, for example, requires that foreign investors deposit a percentage of their investments in local banks for at least one year. By doing so, the Chilean government has managed to prevent speculators from moving their money into the country for a short time just to profit from, say, currency fluctuations. Under the proposed MAI rules, however, Chile would be forbidden to use these policy tools. Similarly, by expanding its mandate to include the liberalization of the capital accounts of its member countries, the IMF would have the authority and power to remove all barriers to international flows of capital.

In effect, giving the IMF control over capital accounts is tantamount to giving it control over the investment policies of national governments. Armed with this kind of mandate, the IMF would have the authority to dictate what kind of investment regulations, if any, a country could maintain and the rate at which a country must reduce and eliminate the regulations it has in place over foreign investment. By exercising these new powers, the IMF would have a veto over how a government deals with sensitive policy issues such as the degree of foreign ownership allowed in a country's newspapers, television, and radio, or whether foreign corporations would be allowed to move into public education and health care. It would also rule on the question of whether the interests of small businesses are to be promoted over that of transnational corporations. While these are the same kinds of policy issues that would emerge under the new MAI rules, the proposed changes in the IMF's mandate would make it the police chief of the global economy.

Although the IMF plan would affect all its members, the most devastating effects would be felt by the developing countries. Over the past two decades, a majority of Third World countries have become dependent on the IMF for funds, especially to offset crippling debt problems. But to receive funding assistance from the IMF, a country must meet certain conditions ranging from increased export production to social spending cuts to the devaluation of local currencies. By exercising control over the capital accounts of countries, the powers of the IMF to compel governments to make these and many other kinds of "structural adjustments" in their economies would be greatly augmented. Even those countries that are not dependent on the IMF for funding would have to submit to its instructions on how to handle their capital accounts. If a country refused to do so, it would not only lose its access to IMF funding but would be in danger of shutting the door on future funding assistance that may be required in times of crisis; it would also risk losing access to private capital, which often requires the IMF stamp of approval.

At the time of writing, these amendments to the IMF's mandate had not been approved. Oddly enough, this matter has become mixed in with decisions on whether or not its member countries are going to make substantial increases in their grants to the IMF in the wake of the Asian financial meltdown. Since the U.S. is by far the single biggest contributor to the IMF and holds 17 percent of the votes on its Board of Governors, all eyes are focused on what Congress will do. Meanwhile, the IMF's dismal track record in stabilizing economies plagued by financial stress hardly inspires much confidence. Indeed, it is precisely the kind of remedies being proposed now by the IMF that precipitated much of Asia's recent financial woes (see chapter 4). What's more, the US$120 billion bail-out package arranged by the IMF will mainly be used to pay back those speculators on Wall Street and elsewhere whose fly-by-night investments did much to destabilize the economies of Southeast Asia.

Bilateral Investment Treaties

The least visible and most elusive players in the MAI shell game are what have become known as Bilateral Investment Treaties (BITs). Simply put, these are investment agreements that are negotiated between individual countries. For countries like Germany and France, these BITs date back to the early 1960s. By January 1997, UNCTAD has reported, there were 1,310 BITs worldwide, most of which had been negotiated by European countries such as Germany (109), the United Kingdom (87), Switzerland (81), France (74), and Italy (54). At that point, the U.S. had concluded 38 bilateral investment treaties with other countries.

Before 1994, these BITs were mainly based on a model investment accord designed by the OECD. But after NAFTA came into effect in 1994, the core elements of BITs focused on investment protection. During this period, the numbers of these bilateral treaties began to mushroom to the point where there are now over 1,600 in existence. The newer BITs, for the most part, feature MAI-like disciplines such as national treatment, a broad definition of investment, expropriation rules, and an investor-state mechanism allowing corporations to directly sue their host governments.

Yet very few people, including Canadians, are even aware that their governments are negotiating these bilateral deals. To date, Canada has already signed twenty-four BITs with other individual countries and is in the process of negotiating another thirty-three. All but five of the signed treaties are based on the new model, which incorporates MAI-like provisions. In negotiating these deals, however, Ottawa has done little to seek reservations or exemptions to protect Canadian interests like the environment and culture. What's more, there has been no real discussion and debate about these BITs in Parliament, let alone in the media.

Today, Ottawa officially calls these bilateral deals "foreign investment protection agreements," or FIPAs. Their main objective is to provide guaranteed protection for Canadian-based corporations operating in other countries. As Ottawa's director-general of trade policy, John Gero, admitted in testimony before the House of Commons Environment Committee, "Canadians [i.e., corporations] come to us and say we want to invest in country X or country Y and their laws are not [good] . . ." In other words, if a Canadian mining company wants to extract silver or copper from Bolivia or the Philippines but finds their laws on toxic waste disposal too restrictive, then it seems that Ottawa will negotiate a FIPA to provide the company with the tools it needs to protect itself against such environmental regulation.

Indeed, the MAI agenda is very much alive and active in a variety of political venues. Like the pea under the walnut shells, it keeps appearing everywhere. For the moment, it looks like the MAI negotiations will remain at the OECD. The critical timeline, say U.S. negotiators Popovich and Larson, will be the next six to nine months. If they are unable to complete negotiations at the OECD by the next ministerial meeting in April 1999, then the MAI will move to the WTO. Canada's chief negotiator, Bill Dymond, seems to more or less agree, but puts more emphasis on the WTO ministerial meeting scheduled for Washington, D.C., in November 1999. Says Dymond, "The MAI will have to come to closure before that meeting: it will either be signed or defeated by then."

Meanwhile, the real architects and chief beneficiaries of the MAI, namely, the CEOs of the major transnational corporations, will not be placing all their bets on the OECD or, for that matter, the WTO. Indeed, the very fact that the MAI agenda is alive and active in other venues provides them with the kind of insurance clause they need. After all, they know there is more than one way of achieving their goal of guaranteed investment protection on a worldwide basis. What's more, if the MAI rules and disciplines become institutionalized in several different political arenas, then corporations will be in a position to make strategic choices about which venues to use for directly challenging and ratcheting down unwanted laws, policies, and programs.

3

Flash Points

On Canada Day, 1998, heritage minister Sheila Copps wrapped up a summit of culture ministers from twenty countries around the world. The participating countries were a diverse mix of the developed and the developing, but they had one thing in common: their governments were deeply troubled by the relentless onslaught of American movies, magazines, television, and music inside their borders and they were seeking ways to protect their indigenous cultures from the forces of economic globalization. No representative of the United States was invited; without saying it in so many words, Copps was making it clear that the problem the ministers most urgently had to address was the aggressive American campaign to force-feed its mammoth entertainment industry to the rest of the world. Group members came out united in their desire to find a way to protect the cultural diversity of their communities and announced that they had formed a permanent network that would meet annually on issues of concern.

Yet only weeks later, when the minister unveiled some timid measures to protect Canadian magazines, replacing existing measures that had been struck down by the WTO, trade experts and the U.S. State Department reacted swiftly to remind the government of Canada that it had signed agreements that make this kind of protectionism highly dubious, if not downright impossible. That same month, Sergio Marchi found himself on the losing end of another trade dispute — this one with huge environmental and health ramifications for Canada — over the gasoline additive MMT. Legislation that Sergio Marchi, minister of the environment, had introduced had to be repealed by Sergio Marchi, minister of trade, when the government backed down in the face of a NAFTA challenge. So embarrassing was this for the minister that the Liberals sent out industry minister John Manley and current environment minister Christine Stewart to face the press and defend the indefensible.

What Copps and Marchi, both on the "left" of the Liberal Party, are learning is that Ottawa can do little to defend Canadian interests in these and other areas because it has already compromised its sovereignty under NAFTA and the WTO. Even without an MAI, big business is well on its way to setting nation-state policy in Canada.

The Ban on MMT

In June 1997, the Chrétien government legislated a ban on the cross-border sale of MMT, a gasoline additive that many believe is a dangerous neurotoxin which also interferes with the diagnostic system that controls a car's anti-pollution devices; MMT at once increases air pollution and potentially delivers a poison to the human brain. While in opposition in the early 1990s, Jean Chrétien had called MMT "an insidious neurotoxin" that could have "truly horrific effects." And in sponsoring the 1997 legislation, then environment minister Sergio Marchi said emphatically that MMT is a hazard to the health of Canadians and to the environment. Canadian auto makers are unequivocal in their statements about MMT. General Motors of Canada vice-president Tayce Wakefield says the scientific proof of MMT's harm to the environment is "incontrovertible and conclusive." MMT is illegal in Europe, California, and much of the U.S. eastern seaboard. The Environmental Protection Agency opposes its use and 85 percent of the gasoline sold in the United States is MMT-free.

The reason the Canadian government used a ban on the cross-border sale, or trade, of MMT rather than an outright health ban is that Health Canada had indicated a need for more research on the product's long-term effects, even though there were some very disturbing reports of its short-term effects on the public's health. Marchi defended the trade ban, declaring that Canada had a "sovereign right" to use whatever legislation it deemed necessary to stop the use of MMT. Whatever the means, said the government, they were still upholding the "precautionary principle" of public health that prevents the use of a potentially dangerous product until its safety has been confirmed.

Enter the North American Free Trade Agreement. For the first time in an international trade agreement, Chapter 11 of NAFTA allows a private corporation to sue a foreign NAFTA government directly if it passes legislation that causes the company to lose profit. MMT is produced by only one company — Virginia-based Ethyl Corp. — and, using this provision, Ethyl launched a

NAFTA challenge against the Canadian government immediately after the ban was announced, demanding $350 million in financial compensation. The suit came before not Canadian courts, but a confidential three-person panel of trade bureaucrats appointed by the two governments. Had the panel finished its mandate, it would have conducted all its procedures in private, no environmental or health groups could have testified before it, and its decision would have been binding on Ottawa.

It never got that far. Legal experts in his department told Sergio Marchi, who had changed portfolios and become minister of international trade, that he was going to lose the NAFTA challenge, costing Canadian taxpayers hundreds of millions of dollars. The federal government had already lost an internal trade dispute when Alberta teamed up with the big oil companies (who love MMT because it is the cheapest way to boost gasoline octane levels to meet legal requirements) to challenge Ottawa's right to ban the additive. This was the first ruling under the new Agreement on Internal Trade (AIT) — NAFTA applied to the provinces — which gives the provinces the right to challenge federal environmental laws if they can be shown to be "trade restrictive."

More important, the government was afraid that a negative ruling on this case would give MAI opponents a powerful new tool, as the MAI contains even broader rights for corporations to sue governments if their interests are compromised than does NAFTA. When he found himself defending the MAI in a February 1998 speech, Marchi had tried to assuage citizens' fears by swearing that he would never sign a deal that allowed corporations to sue the Canadian government for acting in the interests of its citizens. Then in July, realizing that a NAFTA challenge by Ethyl was an example of just that, he could not allow the MMT case to proceed. If the government lost such a case under NAFTA, it would be difficult to sell the similar provisions of the MAI.

So in July 1998, the Chrétien government completely reversed its position on MMT, saying that there is no evidence that the additive is harmful. It repealed the ban on MMT, paid Ethyl almost $20 million as compensation for its costs in the affair and lost profit as a result of the year-old ban, and wrote a letter of apology containing a statement — music to Ethyl's ears — that there is no scientific evidence that MMT poses a threat to human health or the environment. Said a company spokesperson: "It's a very happy day . . . a significant step for Ethyl Corp. and its business worldwide."

This was a shocking abdication of the government's responsibility to safeguard the health of Canadian citizens and their environment and a total reversal of the principled stand it had taken a year before. The government, hoping its backpedalling would head off the bad publicity that a negative NAFTA ruling would have generated, tried to keep quiet about the Ethyl settlement. But the plan was scuttled when a diligent reporter, Shawn McCarthy of *The Globe and Mail*, stayed on the case and exposed the deal the government had hoped to keep in the backrooms. This case was embarrassing for Marchi and the government, but most distressingly, it set a terrible precedent for other corporations to dictate policy to governments in Canada and around the world.

It is not the first time a corporation has attempted to do so. In 1994, giant American weapons-maker Lockheed threatened the Liberal government with a NAFTA challenge when it cancelled the Pearson airport contract signed by the previous government. The same year, U.S. tobacco companies warned that they would launch a NAFTA challenge if the Liberals introduced promised legislation to force the companies to sell their cigarettes in plain packages. In the first case, a settlement was reached between the parties without recourse to NAFTA, although the threat may very well have provided a strong incentive for the government to settle. In the second, the promised legislation simply disappeared, never to be heard of again. And only weeks after the MMT reversal was made public, news of another NAFTA Chapter 11 challenge, this time involving S.D. Myers, a big U.S. PCB-waste-disposal company, was leaked to the Canadian public. When the Canadian government banned exports of PCB waste in 1995, the company was enraged, and threatened the government with a NAFTA challenge. The Canadian government reversed the ban in 1997, refusing to give a reason. S.D. Myers is now suing for $15 million in lost profit for the year and a half the ban was in place.

But the MMT case is the first in the world where a national government has been forced by an international agreement not only to reverse a law it had enacted but also to pay compensation to the transnational corporation that had challenged that law. Under the MAI, potentially every country in the world would be subject to this kind of challenge from every corporation in the world. And citizens would have to foot the bill. It doesn't take a great leap of imagination to foresee a day when corporations build into their business plans a strategy to seek compensation from the public for the cost of complying with health or environmental regulations.

Water Exports

In the spring of 1998, reports surfaced in the media that several businesses had made applications to their provincial governments to export Canadian freshwater for commercial purposes.

The Nova Group of Sault Ste. Marie received a five-year permit from the Ontario government to draw up to 10 million litres of water a day from Lake Superior for export to Asia, and the McCurdy Group of Companies of Gander had applied to export about 52 billion litres of water a year from Gisborne Lake in southern Newfoundland to the Middle East. Ontario has invoked a temporary moratorium on interbasin transfers of water (that is, transfers of water across watershed lines) following negative publicity in the wake of the announcement of Nova Group's permit, but says the federal government has to step in with Canada-wide legislation to make the situation equitable in all provinces. Nova is appealing the cancellation of its permit, pointing out that when the minister, Norm Sterling, granted the original request, he had commented that there was no evidence the project would cause any environmental damage. At first, the government of Newfoundland gave the McCurdy project its seal of approval, citing badly needed jobs, but it is now subjecting the application to an environmental review in response to wide-spread concern about the project.

These two examples are only the tip of the iceberg of an issue that will galvanize Canadians in the next century. The world needs water and Canada has plenty, all flowing north. Transnational corporations are already readying themselves for the global trade in water as governments privatize their hydro-electric and water delivery systems. The next step is massive water exports through tankers, pipelines (some already built to convey natural gas), and water diversion. Robert Kaplan wrote in the July 1998 edition of *Atlantic Monthly* that rampant development is spreading across the deserts of the U.S. Southwest with no regard for their lack of water because the assumption is that all American water resources necessary for the next century will come from Canada, "that shivery vastness of wet, green sponge to the north," in a network of dams, reservoirs, tunnels, grand canals, and supertankers.

Shockingly, our federal government has absolutely no policy on the export or diversion of Canadian freshwater except in NAFTA. Chapter 3 of that agreement establishes obligations regarding the trade in goods and uses the GATT definition of a "good" which clearly lists "waters, including natural or artificial waters and aerated waters" and adds in an explanatory note that "ordinary natural water of all kinds (other than sea water)" is included. When the deal was being negotiated, NAFTA opponents pointed this out and asked the government to specifically exempt the trade in water from the deal. The government argued that under Canadian domestic law, NAFTA does not apply to the trade in water. This is correct. But domestic law does not bind NAFTA panels. In fact, the U.S. clearly established its position at the time. Mickey Kantor, then U.S. Trade Representative, said, "when water is traded as a good, all provisions of the agreement governing trade in goods apply."

"Thus," explains respected trade lawyer Barry Appleton, "in the American view, NAFTA's obligations on water will commence whenever water is traded as a good. This view appears to be an accurate reading of the terms of NAFTA. When water is not traded as a good, it would not be subject to the terms of NAFTA Chapter 3. While water is covered as a good, the NAFTA trade obligations will not apply until water is traded."

In other words, the question is moot until some government in Canada grants a permit to export water. Then water is a tradable good and NAFTA is triggered. Under NAFTA's "national treatment" provision, Canada must exercise "non-discrimination" in the commercial use of our water by investors in all NAFTA partner countries. Private American and Mexican companies would then have the same right of establishment to the commercial use of Canadian waters as Canadians. If Canadian companies are allowed to send supertankers out to export our water, American transnationals cannot be denied the same opportunity. We can only start to imagine the free-for-all that will take place over the next thirsty century.

Now, here's the kicker. Just as a permit to export would make water a "good," any government *ban* on the export of Canadian water also names it as a commercial tradable commodity; again, enter the NAFTA rules. If an American "investor" could show that it had an interest in trading water, it could sue the Canadian government for financial compensation under Chapter 11 — the provision that gives companies the right to sue governments for lost future profit and the one Ethyl Corp. successfully used to bring the government into line on MMT. This is because there was no trade ban in place when NAFTA was signed; post NAFTA, any new law the government introduces is vulnerable to a Chapter 11 challenge. Similar compensation would not be available to Canadian investors.

Back when they were in opposition, Chrétien's Liberals sounded the alarm on this issue. In 1988, Lloyd Axworthy called the inclusion of water in the Canada–U.S Free Trade Agreement (the predecessor to NAFTA) "a covert operation" and promised that when his party formed the government it would introduce a water policy that would give Canadians full control of our water. He said the only way to protect water was to explicitly exclude interbasin water transfers in the body of the actual text of the FTA and that "a unilateral policy statement made by either the Canadian or U.S. government does not change the rights and obligations" in the deal itself.

Once in government, however, the Liberals embraced NAFTA,

which strengthened U.S. claims on our water, and exchanged let-
ters with the U.S. government containing statements recognizing
each country's sovereign right to its water — statements of the
very kind that Axworthy once proclaimed as worthless. His government has been eerily silent on the current controversy over
the proposed exports and has yet to produce the promised legislation to protect Canadian water.

Canadian water resources are at great risk under NAFTA. If
the government succeeds in extending these provisions to a
global MAI, transnational corporations of all signatory countries
will have a similar claim to our freshwater supplies.

Canadian Magazines

In July 1997, Canada lost an appeal to the World Trade
Organization to overturn an earlier ruling that had struck down
provisions used to protect Canadian magazines. In July 1998, a
year later, the Canadian government fully complied with the
ruling, announcing that it would cease using the offending measures and, amid much fanfare to gloss over this total capitulation,
proposed several mild replacement measures that are already
under attack.

The Canadian magazine industry's battle to claim a small
space on the shelves of bookstores and smoke shops has a long
and painful history. Foreign magazines, mostly American,
account for almost 90 percent of newsstand sales. Seven out of
ten Canadian titles don't show up on Canadian newsstands at all
and the trade imbalance in magazines between the two countries
is dramatic: the American industry ships $700 million worth of
magazines into Canada every year, compared with only $10 mil-
lion in exports of Canadian magazines to the U.S.

But that isn't good enough for the American magazine industry and so the U.S. launched a trade challenge, arguing that Canada's policies violated the WTO (which treats culture as simply another commodity, like any widget) by giving preference to its own magazines. The WTO won, and Canada lost the key policies it has used to protect its magazine industry: the 80 percent tariff and excise tax on split-runs (the practice whereby American magazines keep their U.S. content but sell Canadian advertising) and postal subsidies. The WTO ruled that magazines are a "good" and, under the national treatment clause (which forbids a country to favour its own industry), their country of origin is irrelevant. Tax advantages and postal subsidies for Canadian magazines are a clear violation of the WTO, of which Canada has been a cheerleader.

Experts on all sides of the debate and on both sides of the border agreed that this was a precedent-setting decision that would have huge ramifications for all of Canada's cultural industries. U.S. Trade Representative Charlene Barshefsky was jubilant, saying the decision would serve as a useful weapon against Canada's other protectionist cultural policies. The pressure was on for the Canadian government to find "replacement" rules and Copps obliged with an announcement that her government intends to prohibit Canadian advertisers from placing ads in split-runs and will levy fines as high as $250,000 against foreign-based publishers breaking the ban. The government argues that this proposed measure will meet WTO scrutiny because it is aimed at advertising, which is considered a "service" rather than a "good," and the rules for services are less strict than those for goods.

But Charlene Barshefsky disagrees. She says that this is "the same old story" and that Canada is simply replacing one set of discriminatory practices with another. She has promised a trade challenge that trade lawyers say she could very well win. Barry Appleton explains that, even if the Canadian measures appear to apply only to advertising, the end effect will be on the magazines themselves, which, the U.S. will point out, are "goods" covered by the WTO. Another trade expert, Peter Clark, adds, "Anything that treats Canadian magazines differently from foreign magazines is going to run into national treatment problems."

As well, the U.S. may have another fall-back position — NAFTA. Advertising is included in that agreement and not subject to the (weak in any case) cultural exemption. The U.S. could go "venue-shopping" in its challenges to Canadian cultural measures and break them up one at a time. Trade experts point out that direct subsidies — opposed by the magazine publishers themselves, who worry that their political neutrality might be compromised by such payments — are probably the only type of protection not challengeable under these trade deals.

No one is happy with the situation. The Cabinet is split on whether there ought to be any protection of Canadian culture at all or whether it is time to expose it to the global winds of competition. Canadian advertisers are furious; the Association of Canadian Advertisers declared that they may challenge the proposed ban under the Charter of Rights and Freedoms. Magazine publishers have just lost their former protections, which were positive measures and widely supported in Canada, and they know that the proposed replacement measure — a punitive ban — might not stand up to a trade challenge. And privately, many in the cultural community say that the new measure is too negative and that it will prove impossible to maintain a vibrant Canadian industry based on threats and fines.

The federal government is boxed in. It publicly claims to want to protect and promote Canadian culture but it is also committed to economic globalization and international agreements that are designed to radically limit governments' abilities to do any such thing. This most vulnerable of sectors is seriously at risk, but as we will see, the fight over culture, like those over water and MMT, is a flash point for even bigger policy disputes under a global MAI.

4

CASINO POLITICS

In the summer of 1998, it was not so much the failure of Ottawa to stand up to global forces on MMT or water exports or split-run magazines that was on the minds of most Canadians. If anything, the summer of 1998 will likely be remembered for the "diving loonie" and the power that global financial markets seem to wield over our destiny. As the country sweated through the dog days of August, the Canadian dollar plunged to a record low of just over sixty-three cents to the U.S. dollar. Despite declining commodity prices, most Canadian export industries cheered as their U.S. market sales soared, while industries dependent on imports of U.S. goods and services scrambled to stay afloat. With the falling dollar spinning out of control, the floodgates of foreign direct investment into Canada suddenly broke wide open.

In the first quarter of 1998, foreign buyers pumped a record

$7.5 billion into Canada, nearly as much investment as was taken in for the entire year in each of 1997 and 1996. Yet, for the most part, this was not the kind of foreign investment that creates new industries and new jobs. Two-thirds of the foreign capital, mostly American, was used to buy out existing Canadian companies. In effect, the sliding dollar had created conditions for a massive Canada-wide clearance sale, with bargain basement prices for U.S. corporations looking for foreign acquisitions. During the first half of 1998, a record eighty-one foreign takeovers of Canadian companies took place, sixty-nine by American buyers alone. For example, one of America's biggest oil conglomerates, Union Pacific Resources Group, bought out Norcen Energy Resources Ltd. of Calgary, while Pepsico, the U.S. soft drink giant, snapped up Tropicana Products of Montreal.

Most Canadians sense that the dollar crisis is part of a much bigger picture. After all, the devaluation of the loonie came in the wake of a major financial meltdown of the economies in Southeast Asia. Once labelled the "tiger economies," countries like South Korea, Thailand, Malaysia, and Indonesia were viewed as the "emerging markets" and "economic miracle" of the late twentieth century. Close to 70 percent of all foreign investment outside of the industrialized countries of the North was concentrated in the tiger economies of Southeast Asia. But suddenly, in late 1997, the value of these countries' currencies began to plunge, which in turn triggered economic chaos, as millions lost their jobs, prices skyrocketed, bankruptcies soared, and real wages were slashed. The Asian meltdown marked the twelfth major financial crisis since 1973 to threaten a worldwide collapse of the global economy. It was also the worst of them all.

As if by premonition, Jean Chrétien had already talked openly about how nation-states are becoming more powerless in the face of global money markets, in an unusual speech before a meeting of former heads of governments in May 1996:

> International finance knows no borders. Tidal waves of money wash effortlessly backwards and forwards, buffeting interest rates and exchange rates [and disrupting] the best laid plans of governments. These financial waves often seem motivated by quick-changing sentiments or the short-term expectations of the proverbial twenty-eight-year-old trader in red suspenders. When a crisis erupts, a nation-state can seem powerless.

Yet, instead of standing up to these global financiers and insisting that their activities be regulated by governments, the prime minister called for a strategy of appeasement. "We cannot stop globalization," he admonished. "We need to . . . adjust to it." Essentially, this is how his government initially responded to the dollar crisis two years later. Ottawa stayed quiet while adopting a do-nothing policy. Finance minister Paul Martin refused to make any public comments on the tumbling dollar, perhaps for fear of provoking another stampede by speculators in the money markets. All he would do is repeat his constant refrain that "the fundamentals of the Canadian economy are sound."

Although in August the Bank of Canada finally intervened in the money markets by selling off hundreds of millions of U.S. dollars, thereby sending a salvo to currency speculators, it proved to be too little, too late. The central bank's intervention stabilized the downturn for two weeks, but then the loonie took another nosedive. Desperate, Martin quickly backed the Bank of Canada's decision to jack up interest rates. While higher interest rates could have attracted more foreign investment, they also carried the risk of choking off Canada's economic recovery from the recession of the early nineties. What's more, the Bank of Canada's move failed to get at the heart of the problem, namely, controlling currency speculation. Indeed, it became clear at this point that Ottawa had very few policy tools in place to deal with volatile money markets through controls over the inflows and outflows of capital.

All along, the Martin–Chrétien strategy has been to appease the global financiers by assuring them that Ottawa is committed to getting and keeping its public finances "in good shape." By eliminating the deficit (albeit on the backs of the majority of Canadians through massive cuts in social spending) and restoring "fiscal health" to Canada's public finances, Martin and Chrétien expected that they would get the approval of the global money traders. But that's not what happened. In the wake of the Asian meltdown, the currency speculators in the money markets took a run at the loonie, selling off large amounts of Canadian dollars and continuing to drive down its value in comparison to the American greenback.

Not all the blame is to be put on foreign speculators alone. Canadian investors have also been on a buying spree for foreign currencies. According to Statistics Canada, net purchases of foreign securities by Canadians, including both corporations and banks, more than doubled during the first half of 1998 (i.e., $9.9 billion compared with $4.5 billion during the same period in 1997). These foreign purchases by Canadians, spurred on by the fact that Ottawa had increased from 10 to 20 percent the amount of foreign content allowed in Registered Retirement Savings Plans (RRSPs), have put added pressure on the loonie. Now, investment brokers, along with the Reform Party and the Canadian Taxpayers Association, are going so far as to demand that the 20 percent limit on foreign content for RRSPs be dropped altogether, thereby removing one of the few policy tools that Ottawa has to control the outflows of Canadian capital.

On top of all this, the diving loonie produced a thriving business for the foreign exchange traders at four out of Canada's Big Five banks: In the first half of 1998, foreign exchange revenues shot up 30 percent at the Royal Bank of Canada, 15 percent at the Canadian Imperial Bank of Commerce, 24 percent at the Bank of Montreal, and 26 percent at the Toronto-Dominion Bank. These, of course, just happen to be the same four banks that have petitioned Martin for approval to merge and form two mega-banks (i.e., the Royal Bank merging with Montreal, and the CIBC with TD) in order to become bigger players in global financial markets. If Martin approves these mergers, the combined assets of the two new megabanks will amount to 70 percent of all banking assets in Canada — a concentration of economic power in the financial sector unparalleled in industrialized countries throughout the world.

Like nation-states everywhere, Ottawa is caught in the trap of an increasingly unregulated financial system built on excessive speculation. In the past, it was generally recognized that governments had a sovereign right and responsibility to control the inflows and outflows of capital. During the 1920s lending boom that led to the 1929 stock market crash and the Great Depression, the renowned British economist John Maynard Keynes exhorted: "Above all, let finance be primarily national." But today, as we shall see, capital flows move instantly around the world, increasingly unfettered by government regulation, to take advantage of profitable, short-term investment opportunities. The massive deregulation of financial markets coupled with the free market prescriptions of international lending bodies like the IMF mean that most governments simply do not have the powers they once had to control flows of foreign capital. This fundamental problem would only become worse if the MAI rules and disciplines on financial transfers are put in place.

Casino Economy

So why is this happening? The short answer is that the global economic system has been transformed into a casino economy in which most investors have become speculators and gamblers. Instead of buying long-term shares in a company engaged in the production of goods and services, investors now tend to put their money into mutual funds where they can speculate or gamble on fluctuations in prices or the value of currencies (the technical term for this is "portfolio investment," which involves short-term trading in stocks and bonds and currency). Over 90 percent of all currency trading today is for speculative purposes. What this means is that when a foreign investor buys up Canadian dollars, the purpose is not to use this money to purchase factories or import goods or even buy government bonds, but primarily to profit from (or hedge against) fluctuations in the value of our currency. Speculative investment, in other words, has supplanted productive investment as the engine of the global economy.

In this global casino, an average of US$1.3 trillion dollars a day is moved around the world, primarily in the form of speculative investments. Here, as Chrétien's image of the "twenty-eight-year-old in red suspenders" graphically portrayed, basic market power lies in the hands of currency traders. With one keystroke, they can move vast sums of money around the world instantaneously. The computer software equipment available today makes it possible to do twenty-four-hour trading in all kinds of money products. Using digital electronic information, the trading of vast fortunes of cybermoney can be portrayed on computer screens. And the sheer size of global financial operations means costs are substantially reduced. For a mere eighteen cents, for example, it is quite possible to complete any multi-million-dollar transfer from one market to another, in order to take advantage of a profitable investment opportunity.

The fears Chrétien expressed in his 1996 speech were bluntly described by Walter Wriston, the former chair of Citicorp, America's leading financial institution, when he talked a few years ago about the power exercised "by 200,000 monitors in trading rooms all over the world [that conduct] a kind of global plebiscite on the monetary and fiscal policies of governments issuing currencies." Indeed, the US$1.3 trillion that currency traders handle every day far exceeds the combined resources available to the central banks of all national governments, which are estimated to be about US$640 billion. In 1992, in a dramatic demonstration of the power of these speculators, financier George Soros, in order to win a bet with Britain's then prime minister John Major, sold $10 billion worth of British pounds in finance markets for a $1 billion profit; by doing so, he single-handedly forced a devaluation of the British pound and dismantled a new EU-proposed exchange rate system.

It was precisely an avalanche of speculative investment, says Walden Bello from the School of Public Administration at the University of the Philippines, that caused the recent financial collapse in Southeast Asia. In the 1980s, says Bello, the economies of Thailand, Malaysia, Indonesia, and the Philippines grew on the basis of productive investment mainly from Japanese companies. Instead of continuing to rely on productive investments in the 1990s, however, the finance ministries and central banks of these countries put top priority on attracting huge loans and portfolio investments. In the case of Thailand, overinvestment in the real estate market resulted in US$20 billion worth of unsold new properties. Once foreign investors realized the properties were not being sold and they were not getting the immediate return expected, they pulled the plug on their investments and triggered a mad rush of investment withdrawals across Southeast Asia. In 1997 alone, writes Martin Wolf of *The Financial Times*, an estimated US$105 billion in private capital investments, representing a staggering 10 percent of the combined gross domestic product of five countries (i.e., Indonesia, Malaysia, South Korea, Thailand, and the Philippines), was taken out these economies.

This is how the global casino economy functions. Speculators temporarily park their money in markets that offer high short-term returns. At the first sign of trouble, however, they quickly withdraw their money and move it elsewhere in the global market. Since speculators tend to have a herd mentality and follow the pack, fly-by-night capital flows are bound to have an enormously destabilizing effect on a country's economy. Once the stampede starts, there is no way for governments to stop it unless they have measures in place to control capital flows. Although the IMF and the World Bank, following the 1994 Mexican peso crisis, began to recommend that developing countries rely on direct investment for productive purposes rather than more capricious portfolio investments, they still steadfastly refuse to promote (or even allow) the use of capital controls. Yet, Chile was able to avoid the "tequila effect" of the peso crisis mainly because its government requires portfolio investments to remain in the country for a minimum of one year.

Following the Asian meltdown, however, there were signs that some free market advocates had begun to reassess their position on the control of capital flows. "The abrupt reversals in economies that were hitherto deemed miraculous," said the influential business journal, *The Economist*, in January 1998, "have challenged the conventional wisdom that it is a good thing to let capital move freely across borders." Even the World Bank began to shift its position in March 1998, favouring some controls over foreign capital flows.

Financial Surrender

A major factor contributing to the development of this high-stakes global economy has been the massive deregulation of financial markets in recent years. Following the Crash of '29 and the Great Depression, a series of modest measures were taken to regulate national and international financial systems. Like many other governments, Ottawa established its own central bank, the Bank of Canada, with a mandate to control monetary policy. The Bank Act was put in place to regulate Canada's chartered banks; the regulations in the act included reserve requirements, deposit insurance, limits on interest rates, restrictions on the role of foreign banks, and the separation of commercial and investment banking. On the international level, the IMF and the World Bank were established by the Bretton Woods Conference after the Second World War as global financial institutions with certain regulatory powers. Just a few decades later, however, the days of a regulated financial system had begun to disintegrate.

Throughout the 1980s, some of the world's leading commercial banks campaigned vigorously for legislated forms of deregulation in the financial sector. Having saturated their own domestic markets, they demanded that the international financial system be opened up. But it was not until October 27, 1986, that the big breakthrough took place with what was called the "Big Bang" — the London Stock Exchange was suddenly deregulated overnight, opening its doors to both foreign banks and security firms. For the first time, an electronic marketing system was installed and banking institutions were allowed to operate as wholesale dealers and brokers in money markets. The London Big Bang set off an explosion in financial deregulation around the world. National laws that had previously barred banks from international investment business suddenly came tumbling down. The Big Bang spread, and financial markets were opened up in New York and Tokyo. Global corporations in search of capital could begin to shop around in financial markets for better borrowing terms and options.

Long before the 1980s, however, Canada had begun to relinquish its own controls over the inflows and outflows of capital. Under the Bretton Woods system, national governments were allowed to regulate capital flows through such measures as controls on bank loans to non-residents, restrictions on foreign currency accounts, and prohibitions on foreign exchange transactions for speculative purposes. But Canada began to remove its policy tools for controlling capital flows as early as 1951, while many other countries maintained them. In 1975, for example, seventeen industrialized countries and eighty-five less-developed countries continued to have regulatory measures in place to control capital flows. By 1990, eleven industrialized countries and 109 less-developed countries still had the policy tools to regulate capital flows.

But by the mid-1990s, Canada's central bank had all but given up its powers to influence the money markets. Under the Mulroney government, decisive steps had been taken in this direction; in 1991, for example, they removed the requirement that all private chartered banks deposit a minimum level of their reserves with the central bank. In so doing, they effectively stripped the Bank of Canada of some of its revenue base, substantially reducing its ability to be a player in the bond markets on behalf of the public interest. At the same time, the central bank decided to make only limited use of one of its most effective tools for regulating monetary policy, namely, the purchase and sale of treasury bills. Little wonder that the Bank of Canada has recently proven to be relatively ineffective in protecting the loonie.

In December 1997, the Chrétien government made commitments to further deregulate its commercial banking and insurance industries by signing the WTO Financial Services Agreement. The agreement will permit 100 percent foreign ownership of insurance firms in Canada. Legislation will soon be tabled in the House of Commons to allow foreign banks and security companies not only full entry to and rights of establishment in Canada, but also 100 percent ownership of banks and security firms in this country. This foreign influence is being injected into the Canadian banking industry at a time when deregulation is already making many Canadians feel they are being gouged by their financial institutions, and the Big Five chartered banks are using the deposits of their Canadian customers to expand their operations in other countries in order to become major players in global money markets.

Despite the WTO Financial Services Agreement, most of the world's bank assets are no longer subject to regulation by governments. It is estimated that 60 percent of the world's private banking is held offshore in unsupervised tax havens. Says Ian Argell, professor of information systems at the London School of Economics: "The electronic transfer of money offshore has made tax-avoidance a bigger business than narcotics."

Meanwhile, Ottawa has done nothing to control the volatile inflows and outflows of portfolio investment that have risen sharply since 1977. As we've seen, portfolio investment is used for speculative purposes; investors sell minority stocks or bonds at a moment's notice to make short-term investments in another country where the returns are higher. Not only has the Chrétien government failed to introduce effective regulatory measures to curb such flows in Canada, but it even tried to force Chile, during their 1996 bilateral free trade negotiations, to abandon its requirement that portfolio investments remain in the country for a minimum of one year. Furthermore, to add insult to injury, Ottawa provides speculators with a safety net against bankruptcies with its Canada Deposit Insurance Program, which uses public funds to back up all investors, regardless of whether they are involved in productive or speculative investments.

Political Roulette

The reluctance of Ottawa to maintain and increase its controls over capital flows constitutes a serious breach of national sovereignty; without these controls, no nation of people can really expect to determine its own economic and social development. The more an economy depends upon infusions of hot money through portfolio investments, the more crucial it is for the state to take financial flows in hand; otherwise, it is at the mercy of the restless speculators whose business it is to invest for short-term profit and withdraw when they sense trouble on the horizon. Moreover, the economic destabilization generated by these casino dynamics will be firmly entrenched if the MAI and its proposed rules for financial transfers and services are adopted.

These particular MAI rules are designed to protect and enhance the free flow of capital, including portfolio investments. Under the MAI's financial transfer provisions, signatory governments would be forbidden to make distinctions between foreign and domestic capital flows because of the principle of national treatment. Consequently, governments would be greatly restricted in imposing controls on the portfolio investments of foreign speculators. Yet it is foreign investors rather than domestic investors who are the most likely to flee a country in response to currency fluctuations or price volatilities.

More specifically, the MAI rules state that a government must ensure that all capital relating to an investment be "freely transferred into and out of its territory without delay," including "the initial capital and additional amounts to maintain or increase an investment." The definition of investment in the MAI text includes: "shares, stocks or other forms of equity participation in an enterprise . . . bonds, debentures, loans and other forms of debt . . . claims to money." Related to this is also a broad definition of financial services which includes: "money market instruments . . . foreign exchange; derivative products including, but not limited to, futures and options; exchange rate and interest rate instruments . . . transferable securities; other negotiable instruments and financial assets . . ."

In effect, these rules would forbid a future Canadian government to impose "speed bumps" to discourage fickle speculative investments and encourage long-term investments. The speed bumps used by Chile, for example, requiring that foreign investors deposit funds equivalent to 30 percent of their investment in Chile's central bank or adhere to a minimum time limit for all portfolio investments, would be ruled out of order under the MAI. So too would measures often used by governments to prevent a full-blown exodus of capital during times of financial crisis, measures such as imposing limits on converting local currency into a currency widely used in international transactions (like the U.S. dollar) or requiring licences for making currency exchanges.

At the same time, the MAI rules could be used to prevent Ottawa from trying to stabilize its economy by establishing a ceiling on foreign borrowing by domestic banks; withholding government-subsidized insurance for the bank deposits of foreign investors; requiring financial institutions to obtain administrative permission for issuing foreign bonds; imposing minimum maturity periods for foreign bond issues; and setting a less favourable exchange rate for the capital transactions of foreign investors. Now that Ottawa has opened the door to 100 percent foreign ownership in the financial sector, the proposed MAI rules would put a set of handcuffs on virtually any steps that might be taken by a future government to re-regulate the banking industry to serve the public interest.

The latest draft of the MAI does include an emergency provision that permits a temporary suspension of these rules for a government facing financial crisis. But there's a catch. It is not up to the ailing country to decide when it is in financial crisis. Instead, the provision calls for the IMF to make that judgement. In other words, the IMF will determine whether a country's financial situation is serious enough to warrant these emergency provisions. Even if the emergency provisions are granted, it is by no means clear that the ailing country would be allowed to invoke controls on foreign capital flows, simply because the measures taken must be consistent with the IMF's Articles of Agreement. Given the fact that the IMF has traditionally resisted the use of such measures even in times of crisis, and that moves are currently being made to amend the IMF's constitution to increase its authority over the capital accounts of countries, the MAI's emergency provisions are unlikely to be exercised, let alone offer much relief.

In the final analysis, what the MAI provisions on financial

transfers and services will do is provide a set of constitutional rules and disciplines designed to legitimize and protect the global casino economy. Under these constitutional rules, governments will not only be compelled to relinquish what controls they still have over capital flows and be prevented from introducing any new ones, but they will also find themselves playing a game of political roulette when it comes to public policy making. After all, have we not seen Chrétien and Martin gambling on the anticipated moves of the currency traders during the dollar crisis? And what about Marchi, Copps, and Axworthy? Were they not playing the same game in dealing with investment or trade challenges on MMT, cultural policy, and water exports? Every time Ottawa attempts to defend a piece of Canadian sovereignty, not only in economic and monetary policy, but also on a wide range of social, cultural, and environmental policy fronts, it spins the wheel, knowing that its actions could be torn to shreds overnight by the money markets or struck down by corporations using the investor-state mechanism. If governments refuse to play the game, then there are plenty of other MAI disciplines to whip them into line. With this far-reaching treaty, the sovereign activities of nation-states are thwarted at every turn.

5

Cosmetic Surgery

On February 13, 1998, after months of both denying the existence of an MAI and defending it as the necessary next stage in Canada's commitments to a rules-based global economy, international trade minister Sergio Marchi finally decided to answer his critics head on. Up to this point, he had tried to dodge the political firestorm that was growing around the issue by speaking in vague generalities, leading critics to charge that he hadn't even read the treaty and couldn't, therefore, answer the difficult questions they were asking.

But the minister couldn't stay out of the fray any longer. Citizens' groups opposed to the draft treaty had sprung up in communities all across the country and were causing him a great deal of grief. A coalition of over forty national groups had formed, co-chaired by the Council of Canadians and the Canadian Labour Congress, and was swamping the government with petitions and research papers. Many municipalities and several provinces, especially British Columbia, had come out in direct opposition to the MAI, or had at least expressed serious concerns about it, requesting further studies on its impact before deciding whether to endorse it.

The government was finally pressured into holding hearings on the MAI, so throughout November 1997 the House of Commons Standing Committee on Foreign Affairs and International Trade weathered a steady barrage of criticism about both the content of the treaty and the secretive nature of negotiations to that point. The committee obviously agreed with many of the concerns raised by the groups before it because, in its report filed just before Christmas, it advised the government to accept the MAI only if it "fully protects Canadian culture, the environment, labour standards, health, education, and social services."

Marchi's February speech, given in the Adam Room of the elegant old Ottawa hotel, the Château Laurier, was sponsored by Carleton University's Centre for Trade Policy and Law, where Marchi advisor Michael Hart, also one of the MAI's drafters, is a teacher. The speech was attended by many influential academics and business leaders, including Tom d'Aquino of the Business Council on National Issues (BCNI).

Predictably, Marchi castigated the "professional doomsayers" with a "Fortress Canada mentality" who were sidetracking other Canadians with "distortions and misunderstandings," but he went on to make it clear that his critics had hit their mark. Insisting that participation in the MAI negotiations did not commit Canada to signing the deal, the minister declared that he would only sign "the right deal, at the right time — not any deal, any time" and added that if the talks were not to produce such a deal, "we can live without it."

(The minister was also defensive about charges that the process had been secretive and said that his government had consulted widely with the Canadian public, including business and non-governmental groups, on the MAI. A few months later, to prove this point, his department released a list of all the groups the government had met with on the issue; however, the list shows that the meetings with environmental, culture, and labour groups did not take place until well into 1997 — after the MAI had become a public issue — and that the only sector that met with government over the MAI in 1995 and 1996, the years when the basic components of the deal were being drafted, was business. In fact, the Canadian Chamber of Commerce and the Canadian Council on International Business — the international arm of the BCNI — and "member companies" got private government briefings on the proposed treaty in 1993, two years before the government now claims it was even involved in any such discussions.)

Then Marchi outlined what he said was the government's bottom line on what an acceptable MAI would have to contain. In essence, the minister challenged his critics' charges that the MAI would replace government regulation with corporate regulation. He declared that he would "make it entirely clear that legislative or regulatory action taken by government in the public interest is not expropriation requiring compensation"; he would completely preserve government's "freedom of action" to set social programs, environmental law, and culture rules; and he would not abide standstill or rollback requirements that restrict governments' ability to pass future laws. Canada's negotiating team was given strict marching orders to convey these strong positions at the next monthly meetings of the OECD MAI negotiating group.

Yet, when the trade ministers met more than two months later in Paris, the OECD released a new draft of the MAI that would permit none of the safeguards the Canadian minister had promised. Standstill and rollback provisions are still contained in the April 1998 draft. The section indicating that corporations can sue for compensation for government "expropriation" (and measures having "equivalent effect") is untouched. National treatment and most favoured nation status must still be granted to foreign corporations, and the ban on performance requirements is still in place.

Over the summer months, taking advantage of the six-month suspension of talks on the MAI, the Canadian government held fairly extensive consultations with industry, non-governmental organizations, and other levels of government. Their goal was to prepare the new Canadian position heading into the next round of MAI negotiations. At best, what they came up with is only a wish list; there is no guarantee that Canada's demands will be accepted by the other members of the OECD. In any case, however, there are still fundamental flaws in the Canadian position which can best be examined in a sector-by-sector analysis.

Jobs

The Concern

Canadians have expressed serious concerns about the MAI's effects on job creation and labour standards. The ban on performance requirements would prevent all governments (the MAI applies to subnational levels of government as well) from obliging foreign investors to create local employment, purchase local goods, or hire a certain number of minority workers (such as aboriginal workers if the project is on or near First Nations territory). Practices to foster local job creation, like investment incentives, low interest loans, or cheap utility rates, would also be illegal. Limiting government contracts to unionized workers could be argued to be discriminatory to foreign companies that are not unionized. Foreign investors could challenge new workplace health and safety laws as a form of expropriation if the laws could be shown to reduce the corporation's profits; they could also demand compensation for labour strife and strikes.

Legislation used to stem the flight of capital, like requiring severance payments to dislocated workers or requiring a company to remain in the area for a minimum period of time, would be challengeable. And, because governments could not favour local or even national industries in the harvesting of natural resources, many Canadian workers in forestry, fisheries, and mining could be left behind. Finally, the MAI would not allow governments to give Canadians or the residents of a province first access to jobs when they privatize a public service, leaving workers with no guarantee that their jobs won't be moved off-shore.

The Government's Proposal

To address these concerns, the Canadian government supports the OECD's many-pronged proposal to protect labour standards. The first part of the proposal would add a clause to the Preamble of the MAI calling for the signatories to renew "their commitment to the Copenhagen Declaration of the World Summit on Social Development and the observance of internationally recognized core labour standards," such as freedom of association, the right to organize and bargain collectively, the prohibition of forced labour, and non-discrimination in employment. The clause would also recognize the International Labor Organization (ILO) as "the competent body to set core labour standards worldwide."

The OECD also proposes including, in the body of the text,

binding language called "not lowering measures," meaning that signatory governments would agree not to lower domestic health, safety, environmental, or labour measures as an encouragement to foreign investors. An accompanying "interpretive note" would explain that "the parties recognize that governments must have the flexibility to adjust their overall health, safety, environmental, or labour standards over time for public policy reasons other than attracting foreign investment."

The Canadian government supports the OECD proposal to attach the OECD Guidelines on Multinational Enterprises — meant to promote some mild labour, social, and environmental standards — to the MAI "while preserving their non-binding character." Finally, the latest MAI text contains a footnote in the "performance requirement" section (which restricts employment requirements) that states, "Nothing in this paragraph shall be construed as interfering with programs targeted at disadvantaged regions/persons or other equally legitimate employment policy programs."

The Effect

Because the Preamble to the MAI is not binding on the parties, adding a clause on core labour standards is a nice gesture, but meaningless unless accompanied by strong provisions in the agreement itself. A note in the April text suggests the reluctance with which the parties approach this issue at all: "It is the strong feeling of many delegations that preambular reference to . . . labour be limited to one paragraph and that it be as short as possible." Further, it should be noted that the MAI-endorsed ILO has no mechanism whatsoever to enforce standards on its own.

The clause on "not lowering measures" has more potential. However, the parties have not yet agreed to make it binding and, in any case, the annex to the April text recommends that it apply only to "the circumstances of a particular investment," which means that countries could still lower standards to attract investment generally, but not to attract a single investor or investment. The flaw here is obvious: who could ever prove labour standards were lowered for one company? In fact, countries regularly lower their standards to create "investment-friendly" labour and tax policies across the board; this provision of the MAI would do nothing to prevent such practices, while the treaty itself would do everything to encourage them.

In their original form, the OECD Guidelines on Multinational Enterprises are purely voluntary for OECD member countries and regularly ignored; there is no reason to believe that would change once they are appended to the MAI. That the Canadian government recognizes the guidelines' cosmetic nature is obvious. In a summer 1998 discussion paper outlining its position on labour standards, the government recommended that "the guidelines should have no bearing on the interpretation of the Agreement."

Similarly, proposed changes to the "performance requirement" clause are not yet binding. In any case, the footnote would not exempt all, or even most, programs targeted at disadvantaged regions or persons in the MAI — only those that mandate specific job creation goals. There are at least eleven other restrictions on performance requirements that could be construed as interfering with such programs.

And that's it. Every other threat to jobs and labour standards is still in the MAI: the ban on local hiring quotas and subsidies to foster local job creation; the right to challenge new workplace health and safety laws; the inability to stem job-destabilizing capital flight; the loss of control over natural resources and the resulting loss of Canadian jobs; and the requirement that newly privatized public services be opened to global competition from the outset. The MAI is still a major threat to quality Canadian jobs.

Social Programs

The Concern

Canadians are also very worried about the MAI's possible effects on their social programs. The provisions on privatization would allow foreign companies to bid on service contracts such as welfare and workfare and on any public service any level of government decides to contract out. Wherever there is a mix of public and private funding, as, for instance, in child-care and elder-care services, foreign companies could use the "national treatment" provision to challenge the public subsidy as an unfair advantage to the Canadian service providers. The MAI also allows a foreign investor to claim the "best" treatment anywhere in the country as its benchmark. Thus, if one province allows private hospitals, not only would for-profit transnational health corporations gain the right to operate in that province, they could claim the right of entry into every province, even those opposed to privatization.

Any new national government social programs, such as child care or pharmacare, would trigger the investor-state dispute mechanism of the MAI, giving foreign-based corporations in these sectors the right to sue for financial compensation. As well, with pharmacare, the government would be prevented from including a "least-cost" condition to make the plan affordable, as that would be seen as favouring the domestic generic industry.

(A least-cost condition is a requirement that where two drugs are of equal quality, doctors must recommend the cheapest brand, which is usually produced by generic drug companies.) Many aspects of education are being privatized in Canada; the MAI would give transnational for-profit education corporations access to Canadian schools and universities. And government attempts to limit health hazards like pesticides and tobacco would be challengeable under the MAI.

The Government's Proposal

Originally, the Canadian government sought to exclude social services from the MAI through a "country-specific reservation" — an exception taken by individual countries to temporarily protect certain sensitive areas. This move was roundly criticized by health care, education, and social policy groups who pointed out that the term "social services" has no internationally recognized definition; in fact, the U.S. has claimed in the past (under NAFTA) that where such services are not directly and exclusively provided by governments, they do not exist "for a public purpose" and are, therefore, subject to challenge under trade agreements. Further, the government was strongly reminded that as long as "standstill" and "rollback" remain in the MAI, any government reservation is only temporary.

In Marchi's speech of February 13, he took a stronger — and better — stand, promising that certain "ironclad reservations" in the areas of health care, social programs, and education would not be subject to standstill or rollback. "In other words, in these areas, we will not accept any restriction on our freedom to pass future laws, or any commitment to gradually move our policies into conformity with MAI requirements." In trade language, the minister is seeking a full "carve-out" for these sectors, which means that he wants them to be exempted from the deal altogether.

The Effect

It is highly unlikely that the Canadian government will succeed in getting ironclad exceptions for these areas. American MAI critics meeting with U.S. State Department officials in the spring of 1998 reported that the U.S. position on carve-outs of the type Canada is seeking has hardened considerably. Nor is there any indication in the April text that other countries are prepared to drop standstill or rollback or the provisions on privatization. In fact, the new text states clearly: "All delegations agree that foreign investors should benefit from any liberalization [privatization] measure as soon as the relevant law, regulation, or practice enters into force."

The Canadian government is likely to fall back on an annex (which has no legal status at the moment) to the April text in which the former chairman of the OECD negotiating group proposes a clause entitled "Affirmation of the Right to Regulate." It states that a country signatory to the MAI could still maintain and enforce any measure that it considers appropriate to ensure that investment activity is undertaken "in a manner sensitive to health, safety, or environmental concerns," but adds the words, "provided such measures are consistent with this agreement." This caveat eviscerates the rest of the "affirmation" as the MAI itself would still contain all of the offending provisions intact.

The government's proposals to protect health, education, and social services in the MAI are unlikely to be accepted and are inadequate in any case. Transnational for-profit health, welfare, and education corporations could still enter Canada unless specifically forbidden in the MAI. New social programs (called "monopolies" in the text) would still trigger challenges for financial compensation from foreign corporations. And governments would still be confronted with challenges like Ethyl Corp's MMT case if they tried to regulate products hazardous to the health and safety of Canadians.

Culture

The Concern
Cultural groups are more worried about the impact of the MAI on Canadian culture than they are about almost any other recent developments (such as funding cutbacks) affecting their industry. This is because the MAI includes cultural industries in its definition of investment, which means that all subsidies, grants, investment policies, and content quotas to protect and promote Canadian culture are challengeable by foreign investors under the national treatment and most favoured nation clauses. The MAI could prevent the government from requiring that foreign film or broadcasting companies locate in Canada in order to operate here or receive subsidies. Grants to the CBC, the Canada Council, and the National Film Board would have to be offered equally to foreign companies to avoid a lawsuit. Foreign book publishers would have the same right as Canadian book publishers to government subsidies. Foreign newspapers would have the same rights under the Income Tax Act as Canadian owners, who can deduct 100 percent of their advertising costs only if they advertise in Canadian publications.

The MAI would allow foreign artists the same access to compensation for radio play as Canadian artists and put them on the same footing under Canadian copyright legislation. It would permit American-owned magazines the same treatment as Canadian magazines, and the standstill clause would prevent the government from exploring alternatives to the measures recently struck down by the WTO (discussed in chapter 3). If provincially owned television stations were privatized, nothing could be done to keep them in Canadian hands.

The Government's Proposal

Trade minister Marchi takes a firm position on culture in his speech. He stakes out the same "ironclad" reservations as he has claimed for social programs, and says that his government wants to exclude culture from the MAI altogether. (The government of France has also claimed a full exemption for culture but is largely concerned with protecting audio-visual products and would likely settle for a smaller exception than would please Canada.) But in the next breath, Marchi acknowledges the very real possibility that such a pursuit would be "unsuccessful" and says that his fall-back position will be a "country-specific reservation" for culture. Other government officials have said that the OECD is deeply divided on this issue and will likely recommend adopting the WTO's position on culture; to date, Canada has not come out against this proposition.

The Effect

The only effective protection for Canadian culture would be a total carve-out from the MAI, clearly spelled out in the body of the text, but it is unlikely that Canada would be able to achieve it. The U.S. government is opposed to a total carve-out and its entertainment industry sees the inclusion of culture in the MAI as a major goal of the talks and as a payoff for concessions it feels it made in the GATT and NAFTA, where, it claims, "Hollywood was sacrificed." However, the U.S. may yet have to compromise on this issue to save the MAI. There are a number of possible fall-back positions, but, as outlined below, they should all be unacceptable to Canada.

The first is to allow Canada (and perhaps France) to have a country-specific exception that is "unbound" — that is, not subject to rollback and standstill. This would give temporary relief, but even unbound reservations are considered transitional in the MAI and must be renegotiated within ten years. The second is to duplicate the so-called "cultural exemption" in NAFTA, whereby in a "notwithstanding" clause, Canada agreed that if it ever invoked its cultural rights under this clause, the U.S. could retaliate with measures of "equivalent commercial effect," and could do so using sectors unrelated to culture.

The third option — and the most likely one — is to adopt the language used in the WTO to address culture. This is clearly not adequate to protect Canada's interests. The only references to culture in the Uruguay Round of the GATT (which, when concluded, led to the creation of the WTO) are a weak provision (subject to elimination) allowing limited screen quotas of domestic films and some protection for national treasures of historic, artistic, or archaeological value. The WTO itself has no exclusion for culture, and, as discussed in chapter 3, the WTO is the venue where Canada lost important rights to protect its magazine industry. It is also widely expected that the U.S. will soon be launching a challenge to Canada's copyright laws at the WTO. This would be no compromise for Canada, but rather a full capitulation of its cultural sovereignty.

Environment

The Concern

Canadian environmentalists are united in their opposition to the MAI. The national treatment and most favoured nation provisions grant foreign-based transnationals full access to Canada's forests, mines, fisheries, energy, and water resources, and the provisions on "expropriation and compensation" give them the right to sue the Canadian government if it or any other level of government introduces laws, policies, or practices that harm their business interests. The MAI would prevent Canada from putting further restrictions on foreign ownership and control of our energy resources or giving preferential treatment to provincial energy and hydro monopolies. Foreign companies could take control of local water and sewer systems if they are privatized and get around land use restrictions, zoning regulations, and forest clearcutting practices.

Foreign fishing fleets would be given full access to our waters. Aboriginal land claim settlements would have to negotiate with transnational corporations that could demonstrate prior interests in the disputed areas. Promised endangered species legislation would have to take into account the trade and investment interests of foreign investors, and the MAI could be used to prevent the government from imposing an energy tax to reduce greenhouse gas emissions. Under an MAI, Canada could expect dozens more cases like Ethyl Corp.'s challenge on MMT.

The Government's Proposal

In a summer 1998 discussion paper to environmental groups and industry associations, Environment Canada has several proposals to deal with these concerns. As with labour, the government is proposing wording in the Preamble that links appropriate environmental policies with investment to ensure that "economic growth is sustainable"; that reaffirms the government's commitment to the Rio Declaration, including the precautionary "when in doubt, don't do it" principle and the "polluter pays" principle (which places the responsibility for environmental abuse on the corporation); and that resolves to implement the MAI in a manner "consistent with sustainable development, environmental protection, and conservation." The government also proposes to subject the non-discrimination provisions of national treatment and most favoured nation to an interpretive note that limits their application to companies "in like circumstances." Thus governments may have legitimate policy reasons to accord differential treatment to different types of investments.

Canada wants to add an exception for the environment to the ban on performance requirements and would adopt the OECD Guidelines on Multinational Enterprises. As well, the Canadian government speculated on whether the MAI should have a general exception for the environment in the MAI similar to the one in the GATT. They have also proposed using a clause like the one in NAFTA that says that where there is a conflict between the trade agreement and Multilateral Environmental Agreements (MEAs) on specific environmental concerns, the latter shall prevail.

The "Affirmation of the Right to Regulate," already referred to in the analysis of social programs, is given as a safeguard for the environment, as is the proposed provision on "not lowering measures" discussed in the analysis of the government's proposals on labour standards. The government also endorses the OECD chairman's proposal to add an interpretive note to the "expropriation" provision to "clarify that an MAI does not establish a new requirement to compensate for losses incurred through regulation or other normal activity in the public interest undertaken by governments."

The Effect

At first blush, these proposals — which are still just a wish list and far from being accepted by the other countries of the OECD — sound promising. They certainly show that the government knows there are serious problems with the MAI from an environmental perspective. But on close examination, they are clearly inadequate to offset the environmental repercussions of the treaty as a whole.

As in the case of labour standards, adding language on the environment to the Preamble is symbolic and non-binding. The positive message given by supporting the precautionary and polluter pays principles are more than offset, however, by the oxymoronic and ambiguous assertion that "economic growth is sustainable." The proposal to modify the non-discrimination provisions of the MAI with the words "in like circumstances" might slightly narrow the definitions of national treatment and most favoured nation, as it would limit the access rights of foreign investors to similar types of investment areas in another country. Thus, it might be possible to ban a product of a foreign investor if it is the sole producer of that product. (Such a clause in NAFTA might have limited Ethyl's claim for compensation, as there is no comparable company in Canada or Mexico making MMT.) But this is a small modification that doesn't mitigate the true effects of the non-discrimination clauses, which grant transnational corporations far-reaching and unacceptable rights to exploit Canadian resources.

The proposal to add a NAFTA-like exception to the ban on performance requirements is far too narrow, as it would apply to only a limited number of government tools and it adopts language that has been narrowly interpreted in a number of international trade disputes, such as one over Canada's export controls to manage its fisheries (a case heard under NAFTA's predecessor, the FTA). Similar problems exist with the GATT's general exemptions for the health of humans, animals, plant life, and exhaustible natural resources; they have been interpreted so narrowly, environmentalists consider them largely worthless. The suggestion that MEAs should take precedence over the MAI in a dispute would be one step in a positive direction if it weren't for the fact that MEAs, unlike the MAI, contain no means of enforcement.

The problems with the "Affirmation of the Right to Regulate," already discussed in the section on social programs, apply to the environment as well. The addition of the qualifier that only regulations already consistent with the MAI would be acceptable cancels any good the clause might have done. Similarly, the problems with the proposal to add a "not lowering measures" clause to the MAI have been outlined in the section on labour standards. The narrowness of the definition renders it useless to the environment as well.

Finally, on the government's proposal to add an interpretive note to the contentious section on "expropriation": this is probably the clause with the most potential and is the most intriguing. At face value, it might appear to nullify the intent of the MAI's provisions allowing foreign investors to directly sue governments for cash compensation, for its intent is to clarify that the MAI will not set a *new* standard in international law for expropriation purposes. The question must be, how serious is the government on this? If there really is no intent to establish a new set of rights for investors, why not do away with the clauses on expropriation and compensation altogether?

As well, the thorny question of NAFTA comes into the picture here. The MMT and other NAFTA challenges are already setting new international legal standards for expropriation as it relates to the environment. To be effective, the interpretive note proposed for the MAI would have to clearly state that these provisions apply regardless of rulings in other jurisdictions. Yet, when the authors met in early summer with Bill Dymond, Canada's chief MAI negotiator, he said that "the benchmark for the MAI is NAFTA. Chapter 11 of NAFTA is state of the art for us." The government appears to have no problem with the precedent that has been set by the MMT–NAFTA case.

The real story here appears to be about a government attempting to fix the unfixable. It is difficult to speculate on the motives involved; some Cabinet members, like Sheila Copps and Sergio Marchi, seem to be genuinely trying to find ways around the WTO, NAFTA, and now the MAI in order to maintain Canada's standards and sovereignty in key areas of public life. The simple fact is, however, that they cannot succeed within this framework. The government even admits in one of its summer discussion papers that it cannot even consider granting citizens the same right to sue corporations that the MAI gives corporations to sue governments: "It has been suggested that labour unions should equally have access to the investor-state dispute settlement mechanism. However, opening up the investor-state mechanism to special interest groups will further complicate the drafting of the MAI."

In fact, the new April text shows a hardening on this issue. It presents several new options for what a "victorious" country can do if a "losing" country fails to comply with a ruling against it, and it contains another strong proposal that would force countries to compensate other countries for claiming reservations such as social programs or natural resources. In other words, governments could be asked to pay into a general reserve, or "kitty," for the right to regulate.

We must remember that the original drafters of these investment rules — the U.S. and the international business community — intended a "pure" agreement that would allow transnational corporations to dictate their bottom line to governments that have no reciprocal power. In a mid-July meeting with senior U.S. trade negotiators Joe Popovich and Alan Larson, American social activists asked if there was any plan to make the OECD Guidelines on Multinational Enterprises binding on corporations, which, they pointed out, would be the only way to give the guidelines any authority. At this suggestion, the officials burst into laughter. Then, turning serious, they carefully explained that this was not possible but that they welcomed any other, "more reasonable" suggestions.

Despite the government's attempts to retool the MAI, its structure and underlying principles remain profoundly undemocratic. The tinkerers are simply trying to fit a square peg in a round hole. That is not to say that rules are not needed; the world badly needs to bring the rule of law to global capital and establish a framework to control the exponential growth in foreign direct investment. Such rules, however, must be based on an entirely different set of values and priorities, priorities that place the interests of citizens, communities, and the earth at the top of the list. It is time for ordinary Canadians to take leadership in creating these alternatives.

6

GLOBAL CHALLENGES

In the wake of the spring 1998 setback of the OECD MAI negotiations, pundits and journalists tried to take stock of how what some called a "rag-tag" grassroots movement had successfully taken on one of the most powerful institutions in the world. *The Globe and Mail* said that activists in the OECD countries had used the Internet to "kill the MAI." *The Financial Times* compared the fear and bewilderment that had seized the OECD to a scene from *Butch Cassidy and the Sundance Kid*: picture a group of politicians and diplomats looking over their shoulders at an encroaching "horde of vigilantes whose motives and methods are only dimly understood in most national capitals" and asking despairingly, "Who *are* these guys?" Veteran trade diplomats were quoted praising the effectiveness of the campaign and noting that it was a first in global politics. Said one: "This episode is a turning point. It means we have to rethink our approach to international economic and trade negotiations."

While activists who fought the MAI have no illusions about the temporary nature of that "win," there is some real truth to the notion that something new is afoot. Over the last twenty years, as transnational corporations have consolidated their economic and political dominance over the global economy, the role played by governments in the lives of ordinary people has steadily diminished. Some take this as a sign that governments are abdicating their responsibilities and relinquishing power, thus becoming minor players on the world scene. Others say that governments are making conscious choices, using their still-considerable power to transform their national economies — through free trade, privatization, and deregulation — into servants of the global capital to which states are now thoroughly beholden.

Whatever the case, the effect on citizens is the same. A vacuum has been created as governments everywhere abandon the public policy field — a vacuum that big business has gladly and, until very recently, exclusively occupied. But there are signs everywhere that an engaged and aware public is challenging the profoundly inequitable underpinnings of the new order and stepping in to assume the role once performed by governments. Within nation-states and internationally, politically organized citizens' movements are making themselves heard as never before.

Students toppled Indonesia's vile dictator Suharto, the former darling of the global investment community, and challenged the role played by the IMF. The plight of the Ogoni people in Nigeria, whose ancient homeland has been despoiled by Shell Oil, has captured the sympathy of supporters around the world. International campaigns against the child labour practices of global corporations like Nike, The Gap, and Disney have put transnationals on notice that they are being watched and will be held accountable for their actions. Even in the U.S., the centre of corporate power, the labour movement is making a forceful comeback.

The architects of economic globalization know that something is deeply wrong, and that recent events have created a crisis of legitimacy for their agenda. At the May 1998 WTO Summit in Geneva, President Clinton, smarting from the defeat of his fast-track legislation for international trade negotiations at the hands of well-organized advocacy groups in the U.S., warned that governments and global institutions like the WTO had to develop "a dialogue with civil society." At the same event, the prime minister of Norway announced that his government was about to hold a nation-wide inquiry with its own citizens on the ethical implications of globalization.

As they spoke, noisy demonstrators from all over the world made their presence known, as they do now at every such official summit. Whether it is the OECD, the WTO, the annual APEC meetings, the G-8, the World Economic Forum in Davos, or the FTAA, wherever the private sector and governments meet to plan the next phase of economic globalization, citizen, labour, human rights, and environmental groups are there at parallel "Peoples' Summits" to defend their rights and shine a spotlight on the official deliberations.

But within this growing global citizens' movement, there is a recognition that it is not good enough to just say "no" to this anti-human, earth-destroying agenda. Civil society must also say "yes" to an alternative vision, and can no longer stand by waiting for governments to act. There will not be any one answer; rather, we must begin a *process* of national and international dialogue and debate if we are to create a very different future for our common humanity on this planet. In part, this is why, in the fall of 1998, Canadian groups have launched a cross-country MAI Inquiry and search for alternatives.

There are those who do not want to undertake this project. They feel the only goal of resistance is to defeat global trade and investment agreements like NAFTA and the MAI and to implement national policies to insulate their own economies and workers from the winds of globalization. Tempting as this option may be, it cannot work. The world has gone too far down the road of integration to turn back. No one country or society can effectively and single-handedly confront the power of transnational corporations and unregulated global markets. Only coordinated action by countries and citizens alike can bring the rule of law to global capital. Most important, it would be treachery of the worst kind to abandon our brothers and sisters in the developing world now.

The challenge before us, then, is to develop a citizens' agenda to confront the tyranny of global corporate rule at the local, national, and international levels.

Re-establishing Principles

The first task on this agenda is to develop a new framework for looking at investment rules, based on our fundamental rights as citizens in a democratic society. As we have seen, the MAI does not recognize the rights of citizens; rather, it highlights the "rights" of corporations or investors. But corporations are not persons, and from a moral and political standpoint, only citizens as persons can be said to have rights in a democratic society. So by incorporating a body of rules to protect and enhance the "rights" of corporations, the MAI would create a constitutional order for the global economy in which the rights of citizens are subverted, or hijacked, by corporations. Other global institutions, like the WTO and the IMF, are threatening to do the same thing. That's why it is imperative that people reclaim their basic democratic rights, starting now.

The United Nations' Universal Declaration of Human Rights, which marks its fiftieth anniversary in December 1998, provides a useful platform. While the wording may seem awkward a half-century later, the Universal Declaration entrenched many of the basic democratic rights and freedoms of individual citizens, including the right to food, clothing, and shelter; the right to employment, education, and health care; the right to a clean environment, cultural integrity, and quality public services; the right to fair wages, collective bargaining, and the formation of unions; plus the right to participate in decisions affecting these rights. At the same time, the collective rights of peoples, as well as individual rights, are incorporated in UN documents like the International Covenant on Economic, Social, and Cultural Rights and the International Covenant on Civil and Political Rights. Moreover, these rights have been reinforced by declarations coming out of events like the Rio Summit on the Environment, the Beijing Summit on Women, and the Copenhagen Summit on Social Development.

Taken together, these documents embody the foundation stones upon which an economy should be built in a democratic society. The primary goal of economic development, in other words, should be to ensure the basic democratic rights and needs of people in Canada and elsewhere, and the primary purpose of investment should be the democratic development of peoples. From this perspective, the prevailing view among the corporate set that investment is simply a means for maximizing economic growth and profits constitutes a negligence of these democratic principles, and ignores the social, cultural, and ecological needs of individual citizens and communities. It is up to nation-states to determine what their development priorities and investment criteria should be to meet these needs.

In investing their capital, transnational corporations must meet certain social obligations, precisely because capital formation itself is a social process. Simply put, all industrial capital is the product of present and previous generations of labour. Moreover, through the state, society makes it possible for the accumulation and use of capital by providing economic (e.g., roads, bridges, etc.) and social (e.g., education) infrastructure. And there is also an ecological dimension in that the national resources extracted from the earth for energy and production are part of our common heritage on this planet. All this is what's known as "the stored social value of capital." Some ethicists say that there is "a social mortgage on all capital"; viewed in this light, corporations have a debt, an obligation to invest capital in ways that serve the needs of the people and the planet that helped produce the capital in the first place.

According to the 1974 UN Charter on the Economic Rights and Duties of States, it is the role of national governments to regulate foreign investment along these lines. In particular, governments have an obligation to outline national development priorities that reflect the economic, social, cultural, and ecological rights and needs of their peoples. Using these goals as a benchmark, governments can establish a set of performance requirements and criteria for corporations to meet if they are to invest in the country or a particular community. The state also has an obligation to protect strategic areas of the national economy — such as finance, energy, transportation, and communications — by establishing enterprises designed to maintain public ownership and control over these sectors. By the same token, governments have a responsibility to protect sensitive areas of society, known as the "commons" (e.g., the environment, culture, health care, and education), through public services and regulatory measures.

To ensure the public interest in these areas, governments must be free to make distinctions between foreign and domestic investors based on the stored social value of capital. Implicitly, domestic investors participate in a social contract by staying in production, hiring local workers, paying taxes, and retaining profits in the country. In doing so, they contribute to, as well as benefit from, the socialized value of capital. But foreign investors that suddenly appear on the scene have made no contribution to the development of social wealth in the host country. In many cases, foreign firms buying an existing domestic company intend to stay only a short time, yet want to be able to take full advantage of the stored social value of capital generated by previous generations of labour. They also want to take their profits out of the host country. This is why nation-states have a responsibility to impose social obligations, not only on foreign direct investment, but even more so on fly-by-night portfolio investments.

The ultimate objective in re-establishing principles of investment is to bring the rule of law to global capital so that the operations of transnational corporations are made accountable and responsible to the citizens of their host countries. The application of these principles will, of course, vary from region to region and country to country. Not only are there differences between governments as to their role and capacities to regulate corporations, but there are also major differences between countries (and between regions) in their need for capital. A country like Canada has access to a considerable amount of capital, while a country like Mozambique suffers from an acute capital shortage. Disparities in wealth are even more acute between corporations and countries. "What's the difference between Zambia and Goldman Sachs?" asked *The Guardian* newspaper. "One is an African country that makes 2.2 billion a year and shares it among 25 million people. The other is an investment bank that makes 2.6 billion and shares it among 161 people."

Re-regulating Investment

The second task in developing our citizens' agenda is to come up with strategies for re-regulating investment, that is, for reasserting the responsibility of governments to develop and implement new legislation and policy tools to ensure that capital meets the social obligations and principles discussed above. Up to now, we have been concentrating our attention on the impacts of *global* capital movements and on the MAI as a dangerous *global* investment treaty. But the task of re-regulating investment is not just a global challenge. It is a task that must be undertaken in local and national arenas as well. Indeed, it could be argued that there can be no effective reform of global investment rules unless national and local governments also take steps to re-regulate investment and capital flows. Since there is little evidence that Ottawa and most provincial governments are going to make these moves on their own, the challenge now is for citizen groups to work out appropriate investment strategies at the local, national, and global levels.

Local Challenges

The MAI debate here in Canada has opened the door for citizens' groups to take a whole new look at the development needs and priorities of their communities. There is, for example, a growing interest across the country in the movement for community economic development (CED), which emphasizes strategies designed to employ local people to produce goods and services for local community needs. By participating in a CED process, citizens can define development priorities for their local communities, including job creation targets, housing priorities, health care needs, environmental safeguards, education requirements, cultural priorities, and a range of related social objectives.

Based on these community development priorities, citizens can then draft a set of performance requirements for foreign-based corporations on such matters as job quotas for local residents, appropriate uses of technology, and procurement of goods and services from local businesses; pollution controls, rules on toxic waste disposal, and local permission for the extraction of natural resources from the community; and procedures for community reinvestment as well as conditions that must be met if a plant is shut down and moved elsewhere. While in some jurisdictions it may be possible for city and municipal governments to impose these kinds of performance requirements on their own authority, provincial legislation will likely be needed to enforce them.

At the same time, the CED process requires that pools of capital be put together for other community development projects. In addition to government funding for CEDs, local branches of banks and trust companies should be directed to make low-interest loans available for these community development priorities. A percentage of the overall capital loaned by banks and trust companies to regular business clients each year should be earmarked for community development projects. Moreover, to expand the pools of capital available for these loans, foreign-based corporations could also be required to deposit a percentage of their investment in local banks or trust companies.

National Challenges

The MAI debate has also sparked the renewal in Canada of a lively interest in foreign investment issues, a level of concern not seen in this country since the late 1960s. Despite the naysayers, Canada remains one of the world's best long-term investment locations. After all, this country possesses an abundant supply of natural resources, consumer markets, skilled labour, and a relatively safe and stable climate for investment. But if foreign-based corporations want to invest here, citizens should demand that Ottawa impose specific performance requirements. Investment Canada, the toothless agency that is designed to promote foreign investment with little or no conditions in this country, should be scrapped. In its place, a Canada Development Agency should be established with a mandate to implement a national development plan based on economic, social, and ecological priorities. Through this Canada Development Agency, performance requirements would be established for foreign investment on matters ranging from job content to appropriate technology, from worker safety to pollution controls, from food safety to quotas on natural resource exports, from cultural standards to requirements for capital deposits in domestic banks.

In order to regulate fly-by-night portfolio investments, citizens should insist that Ottawa make use of a variety of policy tools. To regain some measure of control over capital flows, new restrictions could be imposed on foreign currency accounts along with a prohibition on foreign exchange transactions for speculative purposes. The Bank of Canada should be instructed to start exercising more influence in the money markets by actively buying and selling bonds and treasury bills. To do so, the Bank of Canada's reserve capacities would have to be replenished by requiring that the private chartered banks deposit a percentage of their own reserves with the central bank. In an effort to curb excessive speculation on money markets, a financial transactions tax (FTT) should be adopted in Canada. This FTT could be applied not only to trading in stocks, bonds, and currencies, but also to options, futures, and derivative contracts. It would also generate additional public revenues that could be reinvested in projects designed to meet national development priorities.

At the same time, a concerted plan of action is needed to channel pools of domestic capital to meet national development priorities. The Alternative Federal Budget (AFB), prepared each year by the Canadian Centre for Policy Alternatives and CHO!CES, contains concrete proposals on how to do so, through public investments in transit systems, co-op housing, waste reduction and recycling, retrofits for public buildings, and not-for-profit child- and elder-care centres. In an effort to redirect the billions of Canadian dollars that flee the country every year for investment in foreign business ventures, the AFB proposes that Ottawa establish an Enterprise Development Bank to provide low-cost debt or equity capital for domestic companies undertaking new job-creating investments that meet national development priorities. Similar measures might also be taken to appropriately redirect a portion of the more than $400 billion in Canadian workers' pension funds, with the consent and participation of the country's labour unions.

Global Challenges

The battle over the MAI has also ignited a debate in international citizens' movements about alternative strategies for re-regulating global capital flows. In anticipation of the OECD meeting of MAI negotiators in Paris in October 1998, citizens' groups from countries in both the North and the South put forth several proposals to stimulate discussion and debate. The proposals reflect a diversity of options: an international set of business standards to be enforced mutually by company self-regulation and government regulation; an alternative set of global investment rules with binding enforcement mechanisms; a global peoples' treaty covering international finance, investment, trade, and taxation.

These are all valid proposals, but if global capital is to be brought under the rule of law, there must be a set of global investment rules grounded in the UN Charter on the Economic Rights and Duties of States. Governments, acting in consultation with their citizens, must be able to enact regulatory measures designed to protect and ensure democratic rights and development priorities. A *global* regulatory regime must be constructed in such a way as to allow national governments flexibility in the use of their policy tools. For example, governments must be free to make distinctions between rules for foreign and domestic corporations; impose performance requirements on foreign corporations; and mitigate the destabilizing effects of fly-by-night portfolio investments through controls on the inflows and outflows of capital (controls which might include the proposed Tobin tax on financial transfers, named after its proponent, Nobel Prize–winning economist James Tobin).

Meanwhile, new global investment rules must also recognize the responsibility of governments to secure control over strategic sectors of their economies (e.g., finance, energy, communications) through public enterprises; protect the commons (e.g., the environment, health care, or culture); and utilize a variety of investment incentives to ensure that foreign-based corporations fulfil their social obligations. If there is to be an expropriation clause, it must be strictly limited to *direct* takings of property by the state. The new rules must *not* include an investor-state mechanism allowing corporations to sue governments directly. Instead, citizens and governments as well as corporations must have legal standing before the courts, and disputes should be settled through the national courts of the host country. If any use is to be made of international tribunals, new institutions would have to be created in accordance with the principles discussed above.

Moreover, these global investment rules cannot be negotiated at either the OECD or the WTO. For all its difficulties, there may be only one political venue where such rules could be properly negotiated, and that is the United Nations itself.

In any case, there is little chance of negotiating a new global set of investment rules unless there is a strong push for the re-regulation of investment by national and local governments. It should be emphasized here that NAFTA poses a major obstacle for Canadians. Most of the national and local challenges outlined above would be ruled out of order under the investment chapter (Chapter 11) of NAFTA. This poses a strategic problem. NAFTA needs to be abrogated if Canadians are going to move forward with this agenda. But in the current political climate, it is highly unlikely that the Chrétien government would invoke the NAFTA abrogation clause. At the very least, Ottawa should call for a renegotiation of NAFTA on a range of hot issues — culture, energy, water, and the lack of protection for the environment in general, plus the investor-state mechanism and the national treatment clause. If satisfactory changes were made on these issues, NAFTA would be effectively gutted anyway. If, on the other hand, there is no willingness on the part of the U.S. and Mexico to renegotiate, then Ottawa would be in a position to serve the six-month notice of intent to withdraw, as required under the NAFTA abrogation clause.

Rebuilding Democracy

The third task in challenging the corporate agenda is to create new mechanisms for increasing citizen participation in and control over decision making on both investment strategies and the re-regulation of investment. It is important to recall that at the heart of the MAI battle has been a struggle for democratic participation and control. After all, the original process that gave rise to the MAI was a highly elitist and authoritarian example of policy making. Not only were the basic components of the treaty crafted in secret over a two-year period in the basement conference room of the OECD headquarters in Paris, but the negotiators from the twenty-nine countries at the table worked hand-in-glove with big business associations and leading corporate executives. No authentic citizens' movements were even consulted, let alone involved, during this period. These are the dynamics that provoked a crisis of legitimacy for governments involved in the negotiations, a crisis which, in part, gave rise to Clinton's call for a dialogue with civil society.

This loss of faith, however, goes much deeper than simply the OECD's mishandling of the MAI negotiations or the failure of governments to consult with their peoples. As we have seen, Ottawa's role in policy making on international finance, trade, and investment, as well as a dozen or more major domestic policy fronts, has been largely hijacked by the special interests of transnational corporations. Increasingly, in this country and elsewhere, people feel that they are no longer governed by democratically elected legislatures but by transnational corporations that are unelected, unaccountable, and seemingly uncontrollable. More than anything else, the MAI symbolizes this new political era of corporate rule. As a result, there is a deeply felt concern among most citizen activists involved in the MAI battle that the task of developing alternative strategies for investment simply cannot be left to governments alone.

Yet the call by political elites for a dialogue with civil society raises another set of concerns. All too often, this kind of dialogue is cosmetic, a display of a government's efforts to consult rather than a true attempt to solve problems. The dangers of being co-opted, therefore, are real. What's more, there are no mechanisms for effective citizen participation in public policy making on issues like investment. Where consultation processes do exist in Canada around other policy issues, they are largely ineffective as far as real citizen participation is concerned. In most other countries, these mechanisms are nonexistent.

With a little social imagination, several creative steps could be taken to develop new institutional mechanisms for citizen participation on issues of investment. For example, just as citizens are elected to school boards in order to monitor the implementation of education policies, why not create regional boards of elected citizen representatives to oversee community investment and economic development plans, using a broad range of economic, social, environmental, and cultural criteria based on community development priorities? Why not establish a national constituent assembly, composed of elected representatives from a cross-section of Canadian civil society (e.g., labour, women, environmentalists, cultural groups, farmers, business people, small producers, professionals, international agencies, and religious groups) to monitor and evaluate positions being taken by Ottawa at the MAI negotiations, the WTO, or the IMF? Why not create mechanisms for citizens to participate in reviewing (and, if necessary, revoking) the charters or licences given by the federal and provincial governments to major corporations and banks, using criteria based on national development priorities?

In the meantime, there is much that you can do to become more informed and involved in these issues. A coalition of more than forty Canadian organizations, representing a broad cross-section of the population, has been formed to oppose the MAI. Most of these organizations have their own groups in local communities, where individuals can plug into activities. And the MAI Inquiry, holding cross-country hearings all through the fall of 1998, provides a concrete opportunity to become involved and meet other concerned citizens. More information can be obtained by visiting the campaign web site at **www.canadians.org**, telephoning the national campaign office at **1-800-387-7177**, or sending a fax message to **613-233-6776**.

As we move into the new millennium, the task of rebuilding democracy may well be the greatest challenge of all. For in this new era of economic globalization, it is primarily transnational corporations, rather than democratically elected governments, that are calling the shots. The time has come to develop and organize a new citizens' politics equipped with the capacities and tools required to effectively confront the emerging forms of global corporate rule and to build alternative forms of democratic governance. With the MAI battle, the seeds of this new citizens' politics have been planted, not only here in Canada, but in a number of other countries, both North and South. The task now is to help these seeds grow into a national and global citizens' movement that is committed to fighting for the democratic rights of people everywhere.

SUGGESTED READING

Following the publication of our first book, *MAI: The Multilateral Agreement on Investment and the Threat to Canadian Sovereignty*, in November 1997, Andrew Jackson and Matthew Sanger published another full-length book titled *Dismantling Democracy: The MAI and Its Impact*. The latter is a collection of valuable articles and essays on the MAI and its effects. In addition to information on these two books, the following list contains various papers, articles, and books that have been written recently on the MAI and related issues.

Appleton, Barry. *Legal Opinion for the Council of Canadians on the Government of Canada's Proposed Reservations to the MAI*, November 1997. Also, *The MAI and Canada's Health and Social Service System* (a presentation to the Canadian House of Commons Standing Committee on Health), December 1997; *The Environment and the MAI* (a presentation to the Canadian parliamentary subcommittee on the MAI), November 1997; and *Legal Opinion, A Comparison of the MAI and NAFTA: How the MAI Differs from the NAFTA*, January 1998.

Barlow, Maude, and Tony Clarke. *MAI: The Multilateral Agreement on Investment and the Threat to American Freedom*. New York: Stoddart Publishing Co., 1998.

Canadian Environmental Law Association. *Presentation to the Canadian Parliamentary Subcommittee on MAI*, November 1997.

Canadian Labour Congress. *The Multilateral Agreement on Investment: A Preliminary Critical Analysis*, by Andrew Jackson, July 1997.

Clarke, Tony, and Maude Barlow. *MAI: The Multilateral Agreement on Investment and the Threat to Canadian Sovereignty*. Toronto: Stoddart Publishing Co., 1997.

Dillon, John. *Turning the Tide: Confronting the Money Traders*. Ottawa: CCPA, 1996.

Dobbin, Murray. *Signing Away Democracy: The MAI and Its Impact on British Columbia*. Vancouver: CCPA, 1998.

Economic Policy Institute, Institute for Policy Studies, and others. *The Failed Experiment: NAFTA at Three Years*, July 1997.

Friends of the Earth (U.S.). *The Multilateral Agreement on Investment and Privatization*, by Mark Vallianatos, 1997. Also, *Reasons to Be Concerned About the MAI* and *The Multilateral Agreement on Investment: Foreign Investment Rules That Would Violate the MAI*, both 1997.

Government of British Columbia. *Submission Regarding the Proposed Multilateral Agreement on Investment* (to the Canadian parliamentary subcommittee on the MAI), November 1997.

Human Rights Program, Harvard Law School. *The Multilateral Agreement on Investment: A Step Backward in International Human Rights*, prepared by researchers and students in consultation with the Robert F. Kennedy Memorial Center for Human Rights, 1997.

Jackson, Andrew, and Matthew Sanger. *Dismantling Democracy: The MAI and Its Impact*. Ottawa and Toronto: CCPA and James Lorimer & Company, 1998.

Mander, Jerry, and Edward Goldsmith. *The Case Against the Global Economy*. New York: Sierra Club Books, 1996.

Oxfam (U.K.). *The OECD Multilateral Agreement on Investment*, September 1997.

Preamble Center for Public Policy. *Writing the Constitution of a Single Global Economy: A Concise Guide to the Multilateral Agreement on Investment*, by Michelle Sforza-Roderick, Scott Nova, and Mark Weisbrot, 1996. Also from the Preamble Center, *The Impact of the MAI on Employment, Growth, and Income Distribution* and *Globalization, the Multilateral Agreement on Investment, and the Increasing Economic Marginalization of Women*, both 1997.

Public Citizen. *The Alarming Multilateral Agreement on Investment Now Being Negotiated at the OECD*, 1996. Also, *NAFTA's Broken Promise: The Border Betrayed*, January 2, 1996.

Robinson, David. *Culture, Communication and the MAI* (a paper prepared for the Global Village or Global Pillage Conference in Winnipeg), March 1998.

Schneiderman, David. *Investment Rules and the New Constitutionalism: Interlinkages and Disciplinary Effects* (a paper prepared for the Consortium on Globalization, Law, and Social Science, New York University), April 1997.

Shrybman, Steve. *An Environment Guide to the World Trade Organization* (a paper prepared for the Canadian Common Front on the WTO), 1997.

Third World Network. *A Commentary on the Draft Text of the Multilateral Agreement on Investment*, by Martin Khor, director, Fall 1997. There are a number of other MAI publications from this source, including *The WTO and the Proposed Multilateral Investment Agreement: Implications for Developing Countries and Proposed Solutions*, 1996.

United Nations Conference on Trade and Development. *World Investment Report*, 1996.

Van Bennekom, Sander. *The Multilateral Agreement on Investment: Regulating Investors or Regulating Countries?* (a paper prepared for NOVIB and the Federation of Dutch Trade Unions), 1997.

West Coast Environmental Law Association. *An Environmental Primer on the Multilateral Agreement on Investment*, Fall 1997.

Western Governors Association. *Multilateral Agreement on Investment: Potential Effects on State and Local Government*, by Thomas Singer, Paul Orbuch, and Robert Stumberg, April 1997.

World Development Movement (U.K.). *A Dangerous Leap into the Dark: Implications of the Multilateral Agreement on Investment*, November 1997.

World Wildlife Fund (U.K.). *The OECD and the Multilateral Agreement on Investment*, March 1997.